GHOSTHUNTING
TEXAS

AMERICA'S
HAUNTED ROAD TRIP

GHOSTHUNTING TEXAS

APRIL SLAUGHTER

CLERISY PRESS

Published by Clerisy Press
Distributed by Publishers Group West
Printed in the United States of America
First edition, first printing

Library of Congress Cataloging-in-Publication Data

    Slaughter, April.
       Ghosthunting Texas / by April Slaughter ; foreword by John Kachuba.
       — 1st ed.
       p. cm. — (America's haunted road trip series)
     ISBN-13: 978-1-57860-359-6
     ISBN-10: 1-57860-359-5
      1. Ghosts—Texas. I. Title.
     BF1472.U6S54 2009
     133.109764—dc22
                       2009028970

Editor: John Kachuba
Cover design: Scott McGrew
Cover and interior photos provided by April Slaughter
   unless otherwise credited.

Clerisy Press
1700 Madison Road
Cincinnati, Ohio 45206
www.clerisypress.com

To my children, Madison and Jordyn,
whose soft little hands and great big hearts hold the world.
You remind me every day of how precious life truly is.

To my husband, Allen,
for constantly loving and supporting me through the chaos.
You are my best friend.

TABLE OF CONTENTS

Welcome to America's Haunted Road Trip

Do you believe in ghosts?

If you are like 52 percent of Americans (according to a recent Harris Poll), you *do* believe that ghosts walk among us. Perhaps you have heard your name called in a dark and empty house. It could be that you have awoken to the sound of footsteps outside your bedroom door, only to find no one there. It is possible that you saw your grandmother sitting in her favorite rocker chair, the same grandmother who had passed away several years before. Maybe you took a photo of a crumbling, deserted farmhouse and discovered strange mists and orbs in the photo, anomalies that were not visible to your naked eye.

If you have experienced similar paranormal events, then you know that ghosts exist. Even if you have not yet experienced these things, you are curious about the paranormal world, the spirit realm. If you weren't, you would not now be reading this preface to the latest book in the *America's Haunted Road Trip* series from Clerisy Press.

Over the last several years, I have investigated haunted locations across the country, and with each new site, I found myself becoming more fascinated with ghosts. What are they? How do they manifest themselves? Why are they here? These are just a few of the questions I have been asking. No doubt, you have been asking the same questions.

The books in the *America's Haunted Road Trip* series can help you find the answers to your questions about ghosts. We've gathered together some of America's top ghost writers (no pun intended) and researchers and asked them to write about their states' favorite haunts. Each location that they write about is open to the public so that you can visit them for yourself and try out your ghosthunting skills. In addition to telling you about their often hair-raising adventures, the writers have included maps and travel directions so that you can take your own haunted road trip.

There is an old song with the line, "The eyes of Texas are upon you," but April Slaughter's *Ghosthunting Texas* proves that at least some of those eyes belong to the dearly departed—ghosts. The book is a spine-tingling trip through Texas' dusty small towns and cosmopolitan cities, from the panhandle to the Gulf of Mexico, and east and west across the largest of the Lower Forty-Eight states. Ride shotgun with April as she seeks out Indian and soldier ghosts at Fort Phantom Hill in Abilene. Travel with her to the Von Minden Hotel where the ghost of a World War II suicide can still be heard dragging furniture around, or to El Paso's Plaza Theatre where several ghosts just won't give up their seats. And who belongs to the disembodied female voice that whispers, "Please help! Someone is burning!" in the Caldwell County Jail Museum? Hang on tight; *Ghosthunting Texas* is a scary ride.

But once you've finished reading this book, don't unbuckle your seatbelt. There are still forty-nine states left for your haunted road trip! See you on the road!

John Kachuba
Editor, America's Haunted Road Trip

Introduction

"THE BOUNDARIES WHICH DIVIDE life and death are at best shadowy and vague. Who shall say where one ends and the other begins?"

—*Edgar Allan Poe*

To some, the idea that ghosts exist is nothing more than a product of an overactive imagination. To others it seems to be an amusing possibility, a deeply fulfilling spiritual experience, or a terrifying everyday reality. Whether you are a devout believer in the paranormal, a skeptic who finds there is a more logical explanation for everything, or simply someone curious about the 'other side,' one thing remains constant—the unexplained has always been among us and continues to evoke fear and fascination in all areas of the world.

When I was eight years old, my family moved into a home where odd things happened almost daily. Initially my experiences frightened me, but as the years passed and I began to seek out an explanation, I learned that fear only made things more difficult. I wanted to know, to understand, to survive those things that scared me the most . . . and I did. It was the beginning of a journey for me that forever changed my outlook on life, as well as the afterlife.

I know that ghosts and spirits exist. I have seen them and heard their voices. I have been touched by unseen forces and witnessed apparitions materialize and dissipate right before my eyes. Being an avid paranormal researcher and investigator, these things have become commonplace in my life and have taught me that just when I think I have it all figured out, I am faced with the realization that I still have a lot to learn. No one has all of the answers, but it certainly is an interesting pursuit looking for them and sharing our collective experiences with others in hopes that we may come across that one experience that turns us into true believers.

I am often asked what it is I hope to accomplish in doing the work I do. Am I looking to convince others that the spirits of the deceased walk among us? The simple answer is no. I am in search of validation of my personal beliefs and am entirely open to sharing that information with others with a willingness or desire to listen. The key to exploring anything unknown is to always keep an open mind and to truly soak up the energy that constantly surrounds you in any given situation. Be aware of your environment and be willing to let it teach you something new.

My husband, Allen, is also an experienced investigator who has accompanied me in my travels and assisted me a great deal in fine-tuning the investigative process. There are several things visitors and investigators alike should keep in mind when they visit a location reported to have paranormal activity.

I always stress the importance of making safety a priority. Whether you are visiting a location on your own or investigating with a group of people, it is imperative that you use your common sense and keep away from areas that are potentially hazardous or dangerous. While our curiosities often encourage us to explore that which has been hidden from us, it is very possible that our experiences can be tainted or even ruined entirely by not heeding caution.

Another important point to keep in mind is that we are guests in these locations, and they deserve our respect. Both the physical and spiritual environments around us are sensitive to our actions, and we need to be accountable for how we conduct ourselves. You might even find yourself welcome to make a repeat visit in the future if those who care for the property are impressed with your conduct. This also helps to ensure other curious visitors will have access as well. What good is a great haunt if we can't all share in the experience?

In all of my travels, I have found it most helpful to go in knowing at least a little history of the place and what activity has been reported there over time. While some people prefer to go in blind, I find I am better prepared for a paranormal experience if I have a slight expectation of what could occur. It is important, however, to keep in mind that paranormal activity is not guaranteed. Just as people do unexpected things in life, those who have crossed over work in much the same way. There is an element of choice that seems to carry over from one realm to the other, and while it may seem disappointing at times, it is important to understand that not everything works on our own personal timeline or expectation. It may take some time before you experience legitimate activity, but it is well worth the wait when it happens! Some of my most profound experiences occurred when I least expected them or when my attention was turned to something else.

Take notes! It is common practice among investigators to carry a notebook with them at all times. Documenting all of the details that you feel are important can later validate your experience as a whole. If others accompany you, interesting correlations may develop in your collective notes. Also, speaking with those who are frequent visitors or caretakers of the property can provide you with some of the more interesting details outside of the recorded history.

One of the most common frustrations among beginning investigators is the notion that they need to spend a great deal of money on equipment before they are ready to get out into the field and gather reliable evidence. Nothing could be further from the truth! It is wholly unnecessary for you to invest money into equipment for investigations when it is fairly inexpensive to get started. Sure, having a thermal imaging camera is nice and can definitely be useful, but it comes with a hefty price tag and rarely produces anything anomalous. You can capture some of the best evidence with the simplest and inexpensive of tools, such as a digital camera, digital voice recorder, and one of the most important tools—the flashlight. I often have the opportunity to work with high-tech equipment, and there is the rare occasion it produces something impressive, but my best evidence has always come from the simple tools I take with me everywhere I go.

Paranormal investigation is my passion, and I find it a privilege to meet and network with many individuals in the field as I learn something new from each of them. It is my hope that *Ghosthunting Texas* is a fun and informative read for you, as it has been such a pleasure for me to write. Many thanks to my friends and family for their endless support and understanding, as well as to those I have the honor to work with when forging ahead into the unknown. May your experiences be as enlightening and fulfilling as mine.

April Slaughter
Dallas, TX

North Texas

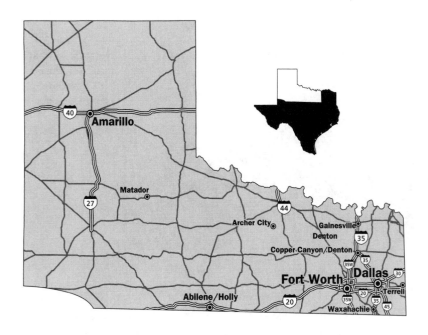

Abilene/Holly
Fort Phantom Hill

Amarillo
Amarillo Natatorium

Archer City
Lonesome Dove Inn

Copper Canyon/Denton
Fort Phantom Hill

Dallas
The Majestic Theatre
Millermore

Fort Worth
The Bull Ring

Gainesville
Hill House Manor

Matador
Motley County Jail

Terrell
Iris Theatre/Books & Crannies

Waxahachie
Catfish Plantation

CHAPTER 1

Amarillo Natatorium
AMARILLO

Natatorium front facade on the 6th Street entrance (April Slaughter)

LOVINGLY NICKNAMED "THE NAT" by locals, the Amarillo Natatorium was first opened to the public as an open-air swimming pool off Route 66 on 6th Street in 1922. A roof was added in 1923 so that it could be utilized all year long. While it provided the community with a valuable source of recreation and an escape from the scorching Texas heat, it survived as a swimming pool only three years when it was purchased by J.D. Tucker and completely converted into a concert and dance hall. The pool was drained and covered with a ten-thousand–square foot wooden dance floor to entertain dancers of the Roaring Twenties. A small hatch was installed in order to access the pool area beneath the dance floor.

The Nat quickly became a treasured retreat for the community as the Depression swept over the United States. A businessman by the name of Harry Badger purchased the Nat in the 1930s, and to keep business and morale up, added a castle façade as well as a café, renaming the structure the Nat Dine & Dance Palace. Several well-known bands and singers were often booked to perform at the Nat. Such notables as Roy Orbison, Little Richard, Louis Armstrong, and Buddy Holly were some of the stars that entertained the patrons and provided an upbeat and fun environment in which to leave behind worry and enjoy a lively evening out.

In 1994, the building was placed on the National Register of Historic Places and in 1995 was deemed a Texas Historical Landmark.

Perhaps the personal struggles of the people trying to survive the Great Depression coupled with the exciting entertainment of the Nat over past decades created the residual energies that still inhabit the building to this day.

Now owned by Jim and Nell Griffin, part of the historic building has been converted into a bookstore while the dance hall area is still occasionally used to host events such as weddings and concerts. Over the course of many renovations to the original structure, people have recounted several experiences of paranormal phenomena. The sound of music playing in the ballroom seems to bring a part of the Nat's vibrant past into the present, as activity has been said to spike shortly after the music begins to play.

In my research of the Amarillo Natatorium, I came across several stories of people throughout the decades who believe the building is haunted because they have had their own personal experiences that defy any other explanation. It is rumored prior owners of the building would often return after having closed it up tightly the night before, only to find that objects and furniture had been moved from their original locations. Lasting only a matter of seconds, apparitions have reportedly been spotted dancing in the ballroom before quickly disappearing into thin air.

These accounts intrigued me so much that I set out with my husband to visit the Nat and hopefully gain a little more insight into its colorful past. The building is immediately distinguishable from several blocks away, as its castle-like façade is unique and does not resemble any other building in the area. The structure sits back from the busy road and is nestled among other commercial properties. Allen and I were immediately excited to be visiting such an interesting historic site. We entered the Nat through the bookstore side and instantly felt at ease in the quaint little shop filled with old books, small sitting areas for reading, and George, the bookstore's resident cat. We had the pleasure of meeting Aaron Baker and his wife Sarah Stone, managers of the bookstore. As we spoke with them we learned that they have yet to experience anything really paranormal, but expect they might someday. They aren't at all worried about the possibility of a ghostly encounter. In fact, they seem to find the idea intriguing and enjoy hearing the stories of others. After all, what good is a bookstore without a good story or two?

"We're here all day, and aren't usually around when it gets late and things supposedly happen," Aaron said. "We've had several people come in looking for ghosts, though most of their attention is focused on the ballroom."

Branden Mann currently leases and manages the Nat Ballroom, which is accessed through the back of the bookstore, and is all too familiar with the spirits that make themselves known in the building. He was gracious enough to allow my husband and I in one Saturday afternoon to see and experience the ballroom for ourselves. I asked him to share with us what phenomena he had encountered in his time at the Nat.

"I have heard so many noises with such consistency over the past five years that I honestly don't even hear or pay attention to them anymore. On one particular occasion, I heard what I thought was the sound of a woman speaking in the same mumbling-type voice you would hear on a Charlie Brown cartoon. I couldn't understand what was being said, but I definitely knew that someone was speaking close by."

Branden is often in the ballroom area working when the sound of footsteps on the upper level can be heard without anyone else being present in the building. While he has no idea who may be visiting or why, he has accepted their presence and continues on with his work despite the sometimes unexpected distraction. He is not at all frightened by the activity and believes that whoever is spiritually roaming the building must be there because it continues to mean something to them.

Allen and I walked around the ballroom to gain a sense of what it must have been like all those years ago when patrons came to the Nat for a swim or for an enthusiastic night of dancing. The ballroom floor is immense, the ceiling high, and there is a slight chill that comes and goes without an obvious source. I walked from one end of the ballroom to the other in silence, all the while feeling as though someone were watching—just as curious about me as I was about them.

The Nat has been visited several times by paranormal enthusiasts in search of validation that it is indeed a haunted piece of history still very active today. Are those who once enjoyed the boisterous music and nights filled with dancing and laughter still drawn to the Nat? Eerie recordings known as electronic voice phenomena (EVP) have captured the sounds of a solitary drum playing quietly as well as the distant melodic singing of an unknown woman. These recordings can be a bit unnerving at first, as it dawns on you that someone may be speaking to you. EVPs are some of the most commonly captured pieces of paranormal "evidence" obtained by ghosthunters. Sometimes these audio clips are recorded in places of ghostly interest, such as the Nat, while others are recorded entirely by chance.

Branden has often allowed ghosthunting investigative teams

and individuals into the building, and spoke with us about the most common phenomena they have reported during their visits. Sudden fluctuations in temperature have been among the most common experiences reported to occur on the upper floor as people have felt cold spots move around them with no apparent explanation.

Investigators have attempted to capture the various reported anomalies and have often found it difficult to keep their video equipment up and running. Sudden and inexplicable battery drainages have puzzled many investigators as they have struggled to conduct the most thorough investigation possible. Whatever is responsible for the strange equipment failure still remains to be seen, but several people suspect it is largely due to the fluctuating energetic environment often experienced when paranormal phenomena occurs.

After spending some time in the ballroom, Branden escorted Allen and me to a section of the bookstore also believed to have

Natatorium Bookstore on the Route 66 side *(April Slaughter)*

activity, where investigators had recorded a disembodied voice on their audio recording devices. We stood where a couple of these recordings had taken place, with a recorder of our own in hand. While we were unable to capture anything that day, it can certainly be said that the entire building has an undeniable nostalgic energy about it. I half-expected to turn around and see someone following closely behind us, listening to us as we discussed the ghostly experiences had by so many in the building.

It is no wonder that the Amarillo Natatorium has garnered so much attention from paranormal enthusiasts and curious locals, as stories of ghostly couples dancing to unheard music on the large wooden dance floor are sure to be a draw for anyone interested in experiencing the unknown. Should you ever have the opportunity to visit the Nat, take the time to enjoy a good book, a good story, and perhaps have a ghostly encounter of your own.

CHAPTER 2

Motley County Jail
MATADOR

**Motley County Jail
exterior
(April Slaughter)**

IN 1876, MOTLEY COUNTY WAS ESTABLISHED
in the Texas Panhandle following a steep decline in the area's buf-
falo population and after the Indians who once called this region
home had been relocated to reservations. Signer of the Texas Dec-
laration of Independence, J.W. Mottley became the county's name-
sake, though the spelling of his name was slightly changed in the
process. Originally, Matador was not an actual town, but was a
working ranch in the county created and managed by Henry H.
Campbell. When organizing the county in 1891, the General Land
Office required that there be at least twenty commercial enter-
prises in Matador before designating it the county seat. Campbell
encouraged several local men to set up one-day businesses to ful-
fill the requirement, and the town of Matador was officially born.
He also became the town's first elected judge.

A growing number of outlaws became such a problem in the
area, that in 1891 the Motley County Jail was erected to help keep

offenders under control. The jail construction provided a much needed resource for men to generate a small income to support their families, as business and money-making opportunities were scarce at the time. The building's sandstone was manually hauled in by workers from Salt Creek, about five miles west of Matador; it was no easy task to complete. Upon completion, the top floor of the two-story structure housed the cells, while the lower level was made into living quarters for the jailer.

Tom Fulcher, a handsome local, was one of the first people to occupy space in the new jail after he was arrested for the murder of a man by the name of Mr. Beamer. The community of Matador was shocked by the arrest, but not nearly as shocked as they would be when Fulcher somehow quickly managed to break free. He was sentenced to life imprisonment for the offense, but never spent any additional time in prison.

A cowboy named Joe Beckham was appointed to become the town's first sheriff, though his service to Matador was less of a priority for him than his outlaw ways. During the Oklahoma Land Giveaway, Beckham left the state of Texas to stake a claim of his own and was replaced as sheriff by a man who eventually arrested Beckham for fraud upon his return to Matador. District Judge Billy McGill ruled that the current sheriff had been illegally appointed, and chose to replace him with someone new rather than restoring Beckham's title. Needless to say, Beckham was not pleased with the situation and decided instead to exact his own justice by arresting the new sheriff along with his deputies and hauling them off to jail himself. As a result, the governor of Texas sent Texas Rangers in to deal with the issue. They eventually caught up with Beckham in the Indian Territory of Oklahoma and shot him to death.

In the decades that have since passed, the Motley County Jail housed a fair amount of offenders until it closed in 1982. Earlier, in 1976, the jail had been recognized as a Texas Historic

Landmark and remains today as a reminder of the frontier history of the state.

On my way out to Matador with Allen, I enjoyed driving through what seemed like dozens of sparsely populated towns. Matador itself has a population of less than one thousand people—three hundred shy of its high in 1940. The buildings downtown sit alongside typical old-town roads, with wider than normal streets and businesses lined up right next to one another. The Motley County Jail sits just beyond the downtown strip, disconnected and solitary.

I can only imagine what life would have been like for those spending any amount of time behind bars in the jail, as they awaited their sentences and served their time for whatever crimes they may have committed. It is quite possible that the wide range of emotions flowing in and out of the jail during its many years of operation have left some residual energy behind that today's caretakers and visitors experience as legitimate paranormal phenomena.

Lance Brooks, co-founder of the research group *Texas Spirit Seekers* didn't initially set out to investigate the jail. In fact, he and his team had traveled out to the area to investigate a private residence, and when the appointment was canceled, case manager James Leslie suggested they check out the Motley County Jail instead. Lance thought it would be a good training exercise for his team, but did not expect it to yield any impressive results.

"We initially thought this would just be a good practice run for our team—an opportunity to set up our equipment and make sure we had our process down. We'd had no reports of anyone experiencing paranormal activity in the building," Lance said. "If they had experienced something, they certainly weren't saying anything about it."

During their initial investigation, Lance was taken aback when the distinctly old-fashioned scent of rosewater caught his attention. No one in the building was wearing anything remotely aromatic, and certainly did not use or have access to anything that would have produced the scent, so Lance took note of it and continued on with the investigation.

"The building smelled dank and musty—the sort of wet stone smell you would expect in a building this old and unoccupied for a long period of time," Lance explained. "The rosewater smell would unexpectedly come and go, especially when we moved from one floor to the next. It was my impression that something was trying to lead us away from the upper floor because as soon as we detected the scent in the jail cell area, we would follow it to the lower floor where it would suddenly dissipate."

In discussing the occurrence with the town historian following his visit, Lance was surprised to learn an interesting fact. A man who had been convicted of a crime and locked up just after the jail opened had reportedly used a type of balmy, rosewater-scented substance to lubricate the cell bars, allowing him to slip through them and escape. The scent was sometimes strongly pronounced, yet subtle and barely detectible at others.

Pleasant scents are not the only thing the members of TSS experienced during their time in the old frontier structure. Members Chris Travis and James Leslie were troubleshooting an issue with a piece of equipment when they noticed something in one of the cells. For a brief moment, they both witnessed what looked like a person leaning out from the bunk and stretching out an arm in their direction. Just as quickly as the apparition appeared to them, it vanished. A short while later, while the group was descending the stairs, the figure of a woman appeared near the bottom step and stood looking at them. She too disappeared out of sight within a matter of seconds.

"I unfortunately did not see the woman's apparition," said Lance, "but Chris and James had seen her twice that evening, and both times on the staircase. The rosewater scent was also very prevalent at the time she appeared, so we're not sure if it is associated with her, Mr. Fulcher, or has some other explanation entirely."

Teresa, another of the group's co-founders, reported that upon entering the gallows area on the upper floor, she began to feel dizzy and sick to her stomach, ultimately forcing her to exit the building in order to recover. No definitive cause for her sudden illness was discovered.

"I hadn't been near the gallows for more than five minutes when I began to feel really sick, and I just felt the need to get out of the building for awhile to get some fresh air. I knew from past experiences that this feeling meant I needed to leave, so I paid attention. After spending some time sitting outside, I returned but decided to spend the rest of the investigation on the lower level of the jail rather than returning to the second floor."

Lance and the TSS team continue to think of the building as an "unexpected hotbed of paranormal activity." Standing as a reminder of all that once was in the rich stories of Texas' past, the Motley County Jail may indeed be home to the restless spirits of those once physically held there.

CHAPTER 3

Fort Phantom Hill
ABILENE / HOLLY

**Fort Phantom
Hill guardhouse
(April
Slaughter)**

FROM A VERY YOUNG AGE, I have possessed a desire
to step out of the present and into the past; to see and experience history and the world around me as it once was. I grew up
fascinated with old and forgotten things. I had much more fun
roaming around abandoned houses and exploring hidden cemeteries in the hills than I ever did playing at the local public park.
Perhaps this is why Fort Phantom Hill first caught my attention. I was pleased to learn that for decades, people have reportedly encountered the unexplained all throughout the sprawling
twenty-two–acre property.

Established in 1851, Fort Phantom Hill—along with three
additional sister forts in Texas—provided assistance to west-
bound settlers by ensuring safe passage through an area that
was home to Comanche Indians. Captain Randolph B. Marcy

sent Lieutenant Colonel J.J. Abercrombie to build the fort in 1849 and construction quickly began. Fort Phantom Hill was never officially given a name—it was originally referred to only as the "Post on the Clear Fork of the Brazos." It has since become known as Fort Phantom Hill simply due to its location on the hill, although many legends exist to suggest that the spirits who inhabit the area today are responsible for the name.

Five companies of infantry were housed at the fort, but life for them was anything but easy. The area was barren and finding a reliable and steady source of water was one of their greatest challenges. I am sure the soldiers would have appreciated access to the man-made lake about two miles south of the fort today. Life was relatively uneventful for the soldiers occupying the land, save for a few encounters with Kiowas, Penateka Comanches, Kickapoos, and Lipans—none of them especially confrontational.

Fort Phantom Hill was not destined to last forever, as it was abandoned in April 1854. Sadly, most of the buildings were set ablaze and destroyed, though no one could determine how the fire began. What was left of the fort following the fire was turned into a way station for the Southern Overland Mail in 1858 and manned by a Mr. and Mrs. Burlington, who lived alone on the property. Colonel J.B. Barry of the Confederacy used Fort Phantom Hill as a base of operations during the Civil War, and in 1871 it served as a sub-post of Fort Griffin, which was located near what is now Albany, Texas.

Today the property remains isolated and nearly deserted, with three buildings still standing and about a dozen stone chimneys scattered about.

Both paranormal enthusiasts and everyday visitors to the ruins have often reported hearing what they believed to be Indian voices and calls coming from several areas within the fort. At times they have felt surrounded by the voices, becoming so uncomfortable that they felt forced to leave. Other stories circulate regarding a man who was supposedly lynched near Fort Phantom Hill for a crime he did not commit; one by one, all of his executioners soon met mysterious deaths of their own. Perhaps the spirits of the Native Americans and this unfortunate individual still keep a close and watchful eye on everyone who enters their territory.

After my discovery of these legends, I was eager to experience Fort Phantom Hill for myself. Allen and I marked it out on our map and set our sights on arriving one blustery winter morning just as the sun came up. As we approached the intact magazine sitting just off of the highway, we noticed a sign reading "No Metal Detectors Allowed." Preservation of the site is the main priority of the Texas Historical Survey Committee, which oversees the property. Whatever remains beneath the surface at Fort Phantom Hill, it is best left undisturbed.

After spending a few moments snapping pictures near the magazine, we crossed the highway and waited for the caretaker to come and unlock the chain that secures the main entrance to the ruins. The sun had been up only for a short while, and the sky was littered with grey and looming clouds. It was a chilly morning and we had bundled up in anticipation of wandering about the grounds in the cold air. After just a few minutes of waiting in the car, a gentleman approached us with a friendly wave and allowed us to enter. Michael Sanchez introduced himself and walked us toward the guardhouse, which is the main building closest to the entrance.

"Sorry I wasn't here sooner. I am a little bit slower on Saturdays."

Mr. Sanchez lives in a home just across the street, and opens the fort to the public every day at dawn, making sure to also lock it up at dusk every evening.

He took a quick look around as we discussed our excitement

in visiting the ruins. Both Allen and I walked around the guard-house and peered into the small barred windows and locked door.

"This building used to be open to the public, but it has since been locked up," explained Michael. "But sometimes if you look in through the doorway and let your eyes adjust, you can see a big owl roosting up near the roof. It's kind of neat to have him in there, making the fort his home."

I stood in the doorway and tried to focus my vision, but there wasn't a lot of light and I did not get to see the fort's resident feathered friend.

I went on to mention that I was interested in profiling Fort Phantom for a paranormal book project, and Michael told us that several investigative groups had made it out in recent months to try and capture activity. Michael has been the caretaker of the fort for over twenty years and has met a lot of curious people interested in learning more about the history of the ruins.

"Throughout all of the years you've spent out here at the fort, have you ever personally experienced anything paranormal?" I asked.

"I was so proud of this one experience," he said. "About a year ago, I walked out of my house when I heard troops calling cadence down in the valley behind the powder magazine. I went in to grab my wife so that she could hear it. When she came out, we didn't hear anything except the sound of cars passing by. When a car passes, that's really all that you hear. She wanted to go back in the house, but I told her to stay and listen. After the cars were gone, my wife heard the voices off in the distance too. I wish I would have written down the date somewhere so that I could go out at the same time a year later to see if I would hear it again. I never did."

Allen mentioned the possibility of residual energy still present in the area.

"What else would there have really been to do out here but practice their marches?" he said.

Michael told us we were welcome to walk the property and spend as much time there as we needed before he left to return home. We had a very pleasant time discussing the fort with him and the possibility that maybe some of the soldiers who once lived here may still visit from time to time. I could tell he was extremely proud of how long he had been at the fort to oversee the ruins, and that he hoped to be there for many more years to come.

Just north of the guardhouse sits an old cistern. Just beyond that is a cannon, which stands alone in an area just before where the officer's quarters once stood. The old stone chimneys and what remains of the foundations are really impressive, and inspired me to imagine what the structures looked like when they were new. I could picture the soldiers as they moved from one area of the fort to another, with a positive liveliness and purpose. I felt a sense of reverence as Allen and I explored and photographed each crumbled structure.

As we made our way to the commissary building, which is still largely intact, I honestly felt as though someone else was following closely behind us. I turned around several times wondering if there were other early morning visitors trailing along, only to find that we were still alone. We had the entire place to ourselves, and we spent a great deal of time just soaking in the environment around us.

There is an old wagon sitting among a patch of small trees and cactus that adds a bit of charm to the frontier atmosphere. Not much sits between the old commissary and the hospital complex due south of it. We took our time to walk across the property, all the while removing small sticker burrs from around our feet.

Allen and I discussed what it must have been like, literally

Fort Phantom Hill grounds *(April Slaughter)*

stuck out in the middle of nowhere. The isolation from others surely must have had some impact on the soldiers who were stationed at the fort. What would these men have done to occupy their time? Fort Phantom Hill was a solitary and quiet pleasure for us to visit. As my husband and I wandered through the buildings and the brush, we held a silent hope that we too would hear the sound of the soldier's cadence carried solemnly on the wind.

Spotlight on Ghosts: Hell's Gates

A small piece of land in northwest Texas near the Lubbock Cemetery has earned a reputation over the past three decades for being an area rife with paranormal activity—resulting from years of reported accidental deaths, suicides, murder, and even Satanic worship.

A wooded area littered with bike and hiking trails, the area has become known as Hell's Gates. Over recent years, it has attracted many people interested in practicing occult rituals. The occurrence of séances and various other attempts at contacting the dead have led many to believe that paranormal activity has been called to Hell's Gates rather than originating here.

Locals and ghosthunters alike have dozens of stories they are more than willing to share with anyone interesting in hearing them. Legend has it that a young woman was once hanged from the train trestle that runs through the property, and that she can be heard crying in the night. Some believe they have captured her apparition in photographs during their investigation of Hell's Gates, often looking as though she were hanging from a rope or simply oating in mid-air just below the trestle. While there is no offlcial record of her existence or death here, her alleged presence continues to attract the curious.

Psychics have often reported the impression of something dark and sinister lurking about the area, angry and defiant, not at all welcoming of nighttime visitors and investigators looking to capture evidence of its existence. Equipment failure is fairly common due to odd battery drainages and rare malfunctions that are often associated with paranormal activity.

The area's atmosphere is said to change almost instantly from calm and serene in the daylight to uncomfortable and frightening at night. While many are attracted to Hell's Gates when the sun goes down, not many attempt stick around to see the sun come up.

CHAPTER 4

Lonesome Dove Inn
ARCHER CITY

**Lonesome Dove Inn
exterior
*(Lance Brooks)***

ARCHER CITY WAS BORN IN APRIL 1881 when a dentist named C.B. Hutto relocated from South Carolina to Texas, built himself a log cabin, and began building a town. The town is named after Branch T. Archer, who was Secretary of War in the Republic of Texas and who actively fought for Texas' independence from Mexico. The population never boomed in Archer City, as it did in other Texas towns, and it has remained a small community.

In 1927, Archer Hospital was erected on the site now occupied by the Lonesome Dove Inn. Dr. T.C. McCurdy built the hospital to accommodate up to fourteen patients, and he remained in practice there until it was sold to Dr. Ted Alexander and his wife in 1944. Dr. Harold Smitson eventually purchased the hospital in the late 1940s and set up his practice until 1957, when the hospital closed.

In 1978, Jay and Patsy O'Neal purchased the old hospital building and converted it into a private residence. A fireplace replaced the emergency entrance, and additional renovations were completed when it was once again sold in 1985 to Bertie Kinsey. Immediately recognizable, the beautiful Lonesome Dove Inn sits in a quiet residential area of Archer City. A wooden sign posted in the front yard bears the name of the inn with quaint lanterns, reminiscent of Old West ways. A short sidewalk leads visitors to the entrance, where majestic white columns stand on either side of the door, proudly bearing a Texas lone star symbol etched in the glass.

Mary Slack Webb and Ceil Slack Cleveland have owned the home since 1998 and have opened their doors to anyone interested in experiencing a little Old West charm. Named after the Pulitzer prize-winning novel *Lonesome Dove* by Archer City native Larry McMurtry, it is beautifully decorated with antiques in every room. McMurtry's books and characters are the inspiration for each of the guest room names—Comanche Moon, Terms of Endearment, Evening Star, and Cadillac Jack among others. Adorning the main floor fireplace mantel are the author's Golden Globe and Oscar award statues. It is said that Mr. McMurtry himself visits the inn from time to time.

Judy McCollough, an associate of mine from Texoma Researchers Investigating Paranormal Phenomena (T.R.I.P.P.), suggested that Allen and I visit the Lonesome Dove Inn after her team had the opportunity to investigate the building on two separate evenings.

"We conducted two investigations at the Lonesome Dove Inn and even spent a night as guests to work in a little photography and EVP work," Judy said. "I had a very strange experience where I felt as though there was a young male spirit trying to communicate with me telepathically. I had never had anything happen to me like that before. I reached my hand out a couple of times where I thought this boy might have been and I actually felt an odd tingling sensation."

Judy also described the images and information she was being given by the boy.

"He said he had died from egg allergies. He had gotten ill, and the first visit he made to the doctor didn't help much as he returned a second time and apparently did not make it. He told me he was eight years old. It was a very bizarre incident. Nothing was captured on recorders we had set up in the room, but just as I stood up from sitting on the sofa, a team member of mine snapped a photograph and a fluid-looking orb was seen in the chair where I thought his spirit might be."

Judy went on to describe several other instances where her team members experienced strange things at the inn.

"One of our team's sensitives, Suni Hoffman, explained that she believed she too was communicating with the spirit of a little boy and that it might have been the same one I had encountered earlier. She felt as though he had been repeatedly kicking her leg in the Desert Rose room."

Paranormal experiences are not limited to ghosthunters at the Lonesome Dove Inn. One guest reported that he had woken late one night to see a woman dressed as a nurse standing beside the bed holding a pillow. When he asked her what she wanted, she offered to provide him with another pillow. When he declined, she left the room.

A family spending the night in the Cadillac Jack room set up a video camera and talked about how they had made their trip to the inn because they had heard it was haunted. When they returned home from their stay at the inn, they reviewed the footage and could clearly hear an unfamiliar and eerie voice order them to "get out."

The beauty and welcoming atmosphere of the Lonesome Dove Inn is enough to attract anyone, but a ghostly encounter is always a draw for Allen and me as we find new places to visit. When we arrived late one Saturday evening, Mary Webb graciously welcomed us in and offered us a tour of the home. As we made our way upstairs, I commented to Mary about the exceptionally wide the staircase.

"During its years as a hospital, they had to carry people in on stretchers with someone holding either side. It had to be wide enough to accommodate that," Mary explained.

After having a quick look at all of the guest rooms on the upstairs floor, I asked Mary if she had ever experienced strange things in the inn.

"One day in particular, I was downstairs in my room at the end of the hall," she said. "I was the only one in the house that day when I heard what I knew were footsteps right above me on the upstairs floor. My son was next door at the time, and I quickly called him over to come and look around the house to see if anyone else was in here. We looked and looked all through the house and couldn't find anyone. That was a little eerie to me. I am familiar with the creaks and noises this house makes, but those footsteps weren't something I could mistake for an old house just making noises."

"I wonder who the spirits are that haunt your inn, Mary," I replied.

"I don't know who they are, but I know that they're nice!" she replied. "They don't bother me at all. As long as they behave themselves, they are more than welcome to stay."

When it was about time for Allen and me to leave, she offered to show us the photographs that the members of T.R.I.P.P. had taken during their investigations. Several photos plainly show a large, illuminated orb that was reportedly captured during coinciding times of activity. Judy McCollough and her team believe that these orbs were a sign that a spirit may have been near them and interacting with them.

While a lot of paranormal researchers disagree on the subject of orbs, it is interesting to note that, in this case, the activity the investigators were experiencing seemed to coincide with when these anomalies showed up in photographs and in correlating locations. Anyone interested in seeing the photos is welcome to do so when they visit the inn.

The house has seen its share of joys and sorrows. When it served as a hospital, it was visited by many people in the midst of trauma or tragedy; but plenty of Archer City residents were also born there. The Lonesome Dove Inn continues to gain popularity among those with a curiosity for the paranormal, and it is sure to generate more experiences in the years to come.

"We have a fun little thing we offer here," said Mary. "Anyone who was born in the house is welcome to come and stay with us on the night of their birthday, free of charge. We've had people take us up on it, too, which we have thoroughly enjoyed! They find it a treat to come and stay in their birthing room."

Allen and I had such a pleasant visit with Mary, exploring the old hospital-turned-inn. So many people have come and gone through the years, it was obvious to me that a little bit of each of them is still very much a part of the inn today. With such a warm and inviting atmosphere, it is no wonder that spirits may call this beautiful place home.

CHAPTER 5

Hill House Manor
GAINESVILLE

**Hill House Manor
exterior
*(Linda Hill)***

I AM ALWAYS A BIT SKEPTICAL when I hear about new places that have gained a reputation for being haunted. The more stories I hear about any particular place, the more I want to see for myself that its claims of paranormal activity are legitimate.

Victoria DuPree, one of our field investigators with The Paranormal Source, Inc., began telling Allen and me about Hill House Manor over a year ago. She and her boyfriend Chris had made the trip to Gainesville from the Dallas area several times to stay overnight in the house, and they truly believed something paranormal was occurring on a regular basis within its walls.

Del and Linda Hill purchased the house in May 2004 as a triplex rental property along with several other homes in Gainesville, but they have no record of who originally built the house. In her research to learn more about the house's history, Linda located a bird's eye view map with a copyright date of 1883, leading her to believe the house was originally built as a small private residence. Several additions have been made throughout the years, and today it's what the locals refer to as the "spooky old house on the corner."

My team and I decided that we would like to book an evening at Hill House Manor to see if any of the supposed ghostly residents would show themselves or communicate with us. We recently had that opportunity, and upon Victoria's recommendation we reserved an entire night at the house. Thirteen of us met in front of Hill House Manor just before sundown, and Linda Hill greeted us all on the front porch. The team waited outside as Linda graciously escorted me on a tour through the house, explaining to me what she believed we might encounter during our time there.

"We have reason to believe that prior to the late 1960s, this home might have been a speakeasy and quite possibly a cathouse," said Linda. "It has become very well known for its EVPs. Our non-corporeal residents are more likely to be heard and not as often seen, but there are times when an apparition appears to visitors in person or on film."

"Has anyone ever died in the house?" I asked.

"I know of one," she replied. "A woman who previously owned the property several years back died here, but there might be more than that. We just don't know. Finding records is complicated, as the street name and house numbering have changed several times in the past."

As we continued the tour, Linda mentioned that she and her husband couldn't seem to keep tenants in two of the house's three livable units for any lengthy period of time.

"We rented the units on a twelve-month basis," Linda explained. "No one ever stayed in the upstairs unit for more than two months, and residents often left the downstairs unit after having lived there no longer than six months. It went on that way for over three years."

The house is now exclusively used for paranormal teams and enthusiasts to investigate, and is no longer used as a triplex. So who is haunting Hill House Manor, and are they responsible for scaring tenants away? We didn't know, but we were sure going to try and find out!

Investigator Victoria Dupree has investigated the home more than half a dozen times, and she contends that something paranormal has occurred on each and every visit.

"I believe there are at least three spirits in the house," she began. "There is a man, a woman, and a little girl. The gentleman seems to be the most interactive. He provides direct answers to questions asked on audio recordings, and I have multiple EVPs of his voice. He speaks with a distinct southern dialect that is consistent throughout all of the recordings. The woman's voice, however, does not turn up on my audio as often. She seems very soft-spoken and not as aggressive as the man."

"Have you ever captured anything anomalous in the pictures you've taken at Hill House?" I asked.

"No, although Linda has a few pictures of what looks like a little girl in the house," Victoria answered. "I have recorded the peculiar sound of a child cooing, almost like whispering, but have never caught an apparition on film."

Victoria went on to describe an incident where she and others had heard the singing of a small child, but upon review of their recordings they did not find any evidence that it had actually occurred.

On the night of our investigation, thirteen of us split up and dispersed throughout the house directly after my tour had ended. Because the home was most famous for its EVPs, we set a block of time to remain still and ask questions in each section in hopes of capturing any resulting responses on our recorders.

Investigator Adam Norton reported that he had put fresh batteries in his recorder, as well as his fiancé Gabriela's, just prior to going in.

"By the time we got to the upstairs bedroom, the battery in my recorder was half-dead," he said. "The batteries in both of our recorders were completely drained before the night was over."

It is a popular theory in the paranormal community that spirits need a source of energy to manifest themselves to the living, often taking that energy from batteries and causing strange drainages. What I find most odd is that even after the batteries placed in various pieces of equipment seem to indicate that this is happening, a short while later their power will be restored as if nothing had ever happened to lower it. While I believe something paranormal may indeed be occurring in an instance like this, I am not convinced that it is a spirit trying to use the energy of a battery to communicate in some way.

As my husband likes to say, "If ghosts actually needed the power from batteries, the Duracell and Energizer manufacturing plants would be the most haunted places on the planet!"

Allen and I also made note of slight variations in battery power throughout the evening, which on occasion coincided with the recording of an EVP.

Around 8:30 in the evening, Adam and Gabriela entered what is known as the "fireplace room," and Gabriela noted feeling an overwhelming sense of love.

"Love you," said a disembodied voice on their recorder.

"We are not scared," said Gabriela. "And we do not want you to be scared."

"I love you. I'm not scared," answered the whispery voice.

Adam thought the voice sounded childlike.

"I always find EVPs creepy when they sound like children," he said.

Chad and Wendy Wilson, a married couple that had just joined the team, accompanied us to Hill House for their very first paranormal investigation. While in the "window room" upstairs, Allen was providing some instruction when he began to feel something touching his right leg near his ankle. He described to Chad and Wendy what he was experiencing and asked them to begin taking pictures of his ankle. No apparent cause for the sensation was evident in the resulting photographs, but Allen noted that it lasted for a good fifteen to twenty seconds. We didn't know it at the time we went in to investigate the house, but previous visitors had actually seen and photographed what looked like a cat's tail in this very room.

When the three of them moved back down to the main level of the home, Chad began to feel as though something was persistently watching them as they moved from room to room. When they approached a dark hallway in the rear of the house, both Allen and Chad began to feel extremely uneasy. For some, such an uncomfortable sensation would result in a prompt exit, but Allen and Chad held their position and then advanced into the hallway. After all, we were visiting Hill House Manor to *find* ghosts, not to run from them.

After a few brief moments, Allen distinctly felt as though a hand had been placed on his right shoulder. He quickly turned around to see who had walked in to join them, but found that no one was there.

After we all had regrouped in the living room on the main floor, we discussed the various experiences of the evening. Each member encountered phenomena of varying degrees, but strange things happened around the entire team during our evening at Hill House Manor.

Overnight investigations of the property occur almost every weekend, and seekers of the paranormal often reserve entire nights to see if they can document anything out of the ordinary. These investigations are also streamed lived over the web via the official Hill House Manor website, connecting curious onlookers with the ghosthunters who brave the night alone in the dark with its ghostly inhabitants.

As we were about to pack up and head home, I thanked Linda and her husband Del for hosting us that evening.

"What do you plan to do with the property in the future?" I asked.

"Eventually we'd like to turn it into something like a bed and breakfast," said Linda. "But as for now, it's just Six Flags for ghosthunters."

Hill House Manor may no longer be a residence for the living, but it seems there are still a few unseen individuals who live there rent-free and who are always up for a visit.

CHAPTER 6

Old Alton Bridge
COPPER CANYON / DENTON

Original Old Alton Bridge
(April Slaughter)

MY INTRIGUE with haunted locations in Texas first began here, at an old bridge no longer open to vehicle traffic tucked away just outside of Denton. While there is nothing outwardly grandiose about the structure or the surrounding area, there is an odd energy in the atmosphere that is almost palpable every time I make a repeat visit.

The bridge was originally constructed in 1884 to facilitate travel over Hickory Creek, and connects the towns of Lewisville and Alton. Built by the King Iron & Bridge Co., the iron truss structure proved an asset to travelers of all kinds including equestrians, those who traveled by foot, and farmers in need of a way to move their stock. The bridge also eventually opened to automobile traffic until the 1970s, when the state of Texas determined that it was no longer safe for vehicle usage. In 1988, the bridge was placed on the National Register of Historic Places and remains intact for visitors to enjoy today, while a new bridge built just downstream handles all automobile traffic for the area.

Old Alton Bridge has long been known to locals as the "Goatman's Bridge," and there are a couple of different explanations of how it may have earned that name. One of them is the story of Oscar Washburn, an African-American goat farmer who settled with his family on property just north of the bridge not long after it was erected. He was a hard-working and gentle man dedicated to providing a good life and living for his family. It is said that a sign was posted on the bridge that read, "This way to the Goat Man's." Being that he was a black goat farmer in the south, his success was not well received by everyone in the community, and members of the Ku Klux Klan were looking to impose their own punishment on Mr. Washburn.

Under cover of night in August 1937, it is alleged that Klansmen forcefully removed Oscar from his home, placed a rope around his neck, and lynched him over the side of the bridge. When the Klansmen went to verify that Oscar was dead, they reportedly found nothing but a dangling rope. His body was nowhere to be found. The Klansmen, in a state of panic, rushed back to the Washburn residence and murdered the remaining family members.

The community suffered a tremendous loss in the tragedy, and rumors quickly began to spread that Oscar's restless spirit would forever guard the bridge and prevent anyone from crossing whom he felt meant to do others harm. This story has survived into the present day, and many people still believe that Oscar's anger keeps him tied to the bridge, wandering the area to ensure the safety of others.

This story, however, is not the only reason the span is called the "Goatman's Bridge." For decades, people have reported encountering a creature described as being half man, half goat. On more than one occasion, visitors have heard the sound of hooves running the length of the bridge as they walked, feeling as though they were being chased away by the Goatman himself. While no photographic evidence exists to support the claims that this creature exists, there are many who will attest that they have seen and experienced the Goatman while out at the bridge and in the woods that surround it.

It was near dusk on my first excursion to the bridge, and I was not feeling well. When Allen and I arrived, I asked him to go on ahead without me to walk around and told him I would be out to join him in a short while. I was alone in the car for only a couple of minutes when I noticed an orange light flitting about the outside of the windshield. For a brief moment I didn't think much of it, and suspected it was merely a lightning bug. After a few seconds, however, the light suddenly stretched into a long, strongly illuminated beam that shot straight up into the air and hung there for several seconds before disappearing. The same phenomenon repeated itself twice more in the exact same pattern within the span of a couple of minutes. As it was still fairly light out, I am confident I would have seen a bug or some other source of the light.

As I exited the car, I gathered my things and joined my husband, who was already exploring the bridge. The incident with the beam of light intrigued me so much, and I wanted to share what happened with Allen before he was out of sight exploring the woods.

"I just had the strangest experience," I said. "I don't know what it was, but this strange orange beam of light just shot over the car."

We spoke about the incident briefly before walking the length of the bridge onto the other side of the river with Jerry Bowers, a good friend of ours—and one of the executive board members of The Paranormal Source, Inc. The three of us were standing in a heavily wooded area just beyond the bridge when we heard rustling noises moving behind us in the brush. It was not a windy day, and we hardly took notice of it at first, thinking it could be an animal skulking around close by. We heard the rustling again, but this time in several places at once all around us. When we went to investigate further, we could find no source for the sound.

Later in the evening, after the sun had set, we set up some camping chairs and began to take a few pictures on the bridge. Almost every photograph captured a view of just how many spiders made Old Alton Bridge their home, as it was littered with webs nearly everywhere you looked.

Allen, Jerry, and I sat down to begin recording some audio. Shortly after turning on our recorders, we began talking aloud to see if we could get some sort of response. If the bridge was indeed haunted, maybe whoever was still lurking about might say something to us.

"Is there anyone here that would like to talk to us?" I asked.

Allen and Jerry also took turns asking questions to the air. We were a bit startled when all three of us heard a woman's voice, seemingly close to us.

"Baby," she said.

There was no mistaking what she said, or that she had been in close proximity to us. The sound of her voice carried such a weight of sadness with it. We were lucky enough to capture this audio on our video camera.

Old Alton Bridge attracts many paranormal investigators and teams all year round, and many of them have reported their experiences with phenomena in almost every form here. Our good friend Lance Oliver, founder of the Denton Area Paranormal Society (D.A.P.S.), has shown us numerous pictures he and his team have taken at the bridge. Many of the photos show odd anomalies, such as several self-illuminated orbs, inexplicable mists, and rod-shaped lights. D.A.P.S. has also had fairly good luck in capturing EVPs at the bridge.

On a repeat visit of ours one evening, a group of teenagers approached us and asked us what we were doing out at the bridge after dark. Allen explained to them that we were there to investigate paranormal activity and asked them if they were local to the area.

"We live not too far from here," said one of the young ladies. "We come out here all the time and usually always have something scary happen."

After a few minutes of chatting with the small group, they left us to our work and headed across the bridge to woods on the other side. Not fifteen minutes or so had passed when the entire group of kids came running back across the bridge.

"What happened?" I asked.

"We were out there in the woods and something came running at us from within the trees," one of the teens explained. "We could hear it. It must have been big because it made a lot of noise and it sounded like it was running really fast toward us. We didn't want to see what it was! It scared us so bad!"

And just like that, they were gone. We hadn't been far from the small group of kids as they went off into the woods and we didn't hear whatever it was coming at them from the dark.

The rest of the evening was fairly uneventful for us until we decided to turn on a K-II meter to see if we could get any readings on it. A K-II is an EMF (electromagnetic field) meter that registers fluctuations in the energetic environment with a series of colored LED lights. While some use the K-II by holding down the pressure trigger on the front of the device with their thumb, we had ours modified with a switch to ensure that we ourselves were not the cause of a false reading. We began to ask questions, and stated that it would be helpful for whoever wanted to communicate with us to flash the lights on the device twice to indicate a "yes" answer and once to indicate a "no" answer.

"Are you male?" asked Allen.

The lights flashed once.

"Are you female?" he asked.

The lights flashed twice.

We asked these same questions several times, and always received the same answers. If there was indeed a woman speaking with us that night on the bridge, we were unable to determine who she was or why she was there. It is interesting to note that many groups have also reported capturing EVPs of a woman's voice on Old Alton Bridge. Some have even captured photographs of what they believe to be a smoky apparition of a woman floating across the bridge.

Does a woman's spirit roam the area looking for her baby? Perhaps the spirit of Mrs. Washburn is searching for the children she once loved and lost. Is there a creature keeping watch over the woods that is half-goat, half-man? Is Mr. Washburn still guarding those who wish to make a safe passage across? All I know for certain is that something or someone is out there at Old Alton Bridge.

CHAPTER 7

The Bull Ring
FORT WORTH

**The Bull Ring
drink and ice
cream shop
*(April Slaughter)***

I HAVE TRAVELED ALL OVER the United States visiting some of the country's most famous "haunts." I have seen and experienced some rather amazing things in the years since my fascination for the paranormal first began. Having the opportunity to travel with my mentors and friends to places I otherwise would never have been able to visit has truly changed my life. While the more well-known places are definitely fun, some of my most treasured memories have been created in places rarely talked about or known at all in paranormal circles.

Sometimes, I come across a place that doesn't have a reputation for being haunted at all, a place that speaks to me and sits quietly in the background as if it were waiting for me to discover it. I have found many of these places over the years; one in particular is the Bull Ring in the historic Fort Worth Stockyards, an area rich in history and perfectly primed for more than its fair share of ghost stories.

Over the span of twenty-four years—from 1866 to 1890—more than four million head of cattle came through Fort Worth as drovers pushed their herds up the Chisholm Trail. The city quickly became known as "Cowtown" and was the last chance for the men to rest and gather their supplies before crossing the Red River into Indian Territory. A rough-and-tumble part of town just south of the courthouse became famously known as "Hell's Half Acre," as it had a reputation for attracting the more violent and lawless type of crowd.

Business was good in the Stockyards, however, despite having suffered through drought and fires that resulted in large amounts of structural damage and the death of many livestock. Success continued through both World Wars, but eventually sales slowed as trucking replaced the railways as a primary means of shipping cattle to their destinations.

The North Fort Worth Historical Society, established in 1976, sought to preserve the history of Cowtown by working to restore much of what was deteriorating in the city. That same year, the Fort Worth Stockyards National Historical District was also established. Most of what might have been lost has undergone restoration, making it one of the most popular tourist destinations in Texas today.

One sunny spring afternoon, Allen and I were visiting the Stockyards to research a couple of other locations in the area. The streets were lined with cars, and there were so many people walking the sidewalks it was nearly impossible to get anywhere quickly. We had been in town for an hour or so when we stopped into the General Store to take a look around. I bought a few little things for my kids and asked the young man at the register if he knew where I could get a cup of coffee.

"Just down the street, there is the Bull Ring. If you're looking for a good cup of coffee, that would be the place to go," he said.

It took us only a couple of minutes to reach the entrance, and as we stepped inside Allen and I found ourselves instantly smitten with the place. A large wooden Dr. Pepper sign hung on the wall just behind the long beverage counter, and you'd be hard-pressed to find a section of the building that wasn't covered in art or odd, antique trinkets.

I stepped up to order our coffees, and as the lady behind the counter was preparing them I suddenly felt the urge to ask her something.

"You wouldn't happen to have any ghosts in this building, would you?"

She paused for a brief moment and replied, "Actually, we do."

Honestly, I was half-joking when I asked and I certainly did not expect her to give me the answer she did.

"Really?" I asked. "Would you mind telling me about them?"

I handed her my business card and introduced myself. She told me her name was Charlene Lindstrom and that her parents, Mr. and Mrs. A.C. Cook, owned the building. They had purchased the property in 2000 and spent three years painstakingly restoring it, opening it to the public in 2003. For years the building had housed a small tailoring business run by an elderly Jewish couple, Mike and Jenny Bornstein, but now it served as a place to grab a soda or beer on-the-go, have an ice cream cone, or enjoy a nice glass of wine.

"You're probably going to think I am crazy, but I know there is a man that lives in this building," she said. "Bill and I have heard him walking around up here when we were down in the basement."

Bill Mackey is a good friend of Charlene's who helps manage the Bull Ring. As we were introduced, he began to tell Allen and me that he was a believer in paranormal phenomena and that he knew without a doubt that someone (maybe even several

people) haunted the building. Like Charlene, Bill also acknowledged that he had witnessed the presence of a man in the building, as had several others over the years. As my husband and I
were growing short on time, I didn't yet have the opportunity to
inquire further about the resident spirit. I assured both Charlene and Bill that I would return soon to discuss the ghost more
with them when I had more time to sit down and hear their
stories.

"You have to see our basement before you go," said Bill. "It
used to be all boarded up, and I can tell you that it has a completely different atmosphere down there."

He escorted Allen and me down the stairwell at the rear of
the building into the basement. It was as if we had stepped into
an entirely different time. Artwork and old photographs were
everywhere, and writing on the concrete wall read, "If you can't
pay, don't play,"—reminiscent of a time when not being able to
pay off your bets might have landed you in a very dangerous
situation with your fellow gamblers.

Several people were running about, preparing for a wed-
ding reception being held in the building later that evening. We
didn't want to be in the way, so we took a few photographs and
asked to set up a time when we could come back in.

"You and your team should come out to investigate the Bull
Ring sometime," said Charlene. "We'd love to have you. No one
else has ever been allowed in to do that before, and I'd be interested to see what y'all would come up with."

"We'd love that!" I said. "Let's set it up."

As Allen and I left, we talked about how surprised we were to
have found a potentially fantastic location completely by chance.
The Bull Ring had not previously been anywhere on our list of
places to visit for the book, but now we could hardly wait to get
back and learn more—and all because I had to have a cup of
coffee!

In the days that followed our first visit to the Bull Ring, Charlene, Bill, and I kept in contact and I began to learn a lot more about the building. It was originally a tavern constructed in 1910 by William T. Cooper (aka "Buck"). In the decades since, it has served as everything from a bar, to gambling hall and speakeasy, a diner, a tailoring shop, and now as a place to grab a drink and enjoy an impressive collection of original art. A.C. Cook has spent years gathering over one thousand pieces by Texas artists who completed works between 1865 and 1965—many of them coveted by other art collectors.

Before I knew it, Allen and I were in the Bull Ring with a small group of investigators listening to Bill has he began to tell us stories of strange occurrences he had experienced in his time employed there.

"Charlene and I were in the basement one afternoon having a late lunch, and no one else was in the building," he began. "Both she and I heard the distinct sound of heavy footsteps walking above us from one side of the building to the other, which is impossible if you look at where the counter sits. Whoever it was would have had to walk straight through it as if it weren't even there."

"Just a few days ago, something else happened I can't explain," he continued. "Knowing this used to be a gambling hall, I took a deck of cards and I dealt out two hands on one of the basement tables. I laid the cards faced down, one hand right across from the other, and placed the deck neatly stacked in the middle of the table. I checked both hands and wrote down what they were just to see if they would change. The next morning when I came back, the cards were the same but the deck in the middle had been fanned out. No one else had been in the building since I left."

After hearing about all of the different experiences that seemed to center around the basement, we decided it would be best to set up most of our equipment there. Bill made sure all of the doors were locked so that we would not be interrupted. The lights went out, and the investigation began.

Only minutes in, I was chatting with fellow investigator Adam Norton when Allen's recorder caught the first of many EVPs we would eventually obtain throughout the evening. Adam and I were discussing updates to The Paranormal Source website when what seemed to be another woman's voice joined the conversation.

"That's nice," she said.

Not even a minute later, a female voice was also heard humming a short tune while Adam's fiancé Gabriella was asking a series of questions.

Normally, genuine EVPs are few and far between. They do not occur in every location and can be quite difficult to catch. A common mistake among investigators is whispering during investigations, which can make the review of the audio confusing. Each time a sound was heard or made among our group that we were responsible for, we made sure to call it out so that it would be identified properly on the recorders. We were definitely attracting the attention of someone unseen, and they were doing really well in responding to us.

For a short time, everyone fell quiet to see if we would see or hear anything unusual. Sudden onsets of temperature changes began to swirl around various members of the group. The basement is a fully functional part of the building, and the heating system was continually running. The cold spots would appear and just as quickly disappear. At one point, deeply cold air seemed to hover between two of the group members for several seconds.

Sometimes I will seek validation that someone unseen is with us by asking them to repeat a series of knocks, whether it be on a wall or a piece of furniture. I tapped a few times on the wooden table I was sitting at, and we all anxiously awaited a response. None came—at least not immediately. Approximately two to three minutes later, however, the same pattern I had tapped on the table was heard by several of us on one of the tables nearby that no one was sitting at.

Adam told me that he had been watching an area near the basement exit door, and had repeatedly seen quick, shadowy movements. I was curious about what could be causing them, so I walked over to the door in hopes of seeing them as well. Immediately after sitting down alone at the bar area near the door, several team members closer to the stairwell said they had just heard two or more people conversing on the floor above us. While I had not heard it, most of the others had. Bill thought it may have been Charlene coming to see if we had experienced anything interesting, and that she might have someone with her. He and Allen decided to go upstairs to check it out, but upon inspection found the entrance door still locked and no one in the building besides the team. I was curious about whether or not the voices would show up on the audio recordings, and was absolutely thrilled to hear them on playback! What was being said could not be deciphered, but voices were indeed captured.

Investigator Victoria Dupree was surprised when her stool was suddenly pulled slightly away from the bar.

"Something just pulled my stool back," she said calmly. All of us kept our attention on her in hopes that the action might be repeated. It was not.

All throughout the evening, we received some auditory response to nearly every question we asked. Hours upon hours of reviewing the recorders produced a record number of EVPs from one location for the team.

As the clock struck 1:00 A.M., the team was growing a bit tired and we decided to start packing everything up in preparation to leave. We thanked Bill for his time and graciousness, and promised to be in touch with what we found during our initial investigation of the building.

As anyone who often ghost hunts will tell you, reviewing data takes a great deal of time and attention. Over the course of a week following the investigation, every member of our team pored over hours and hours of audio and video. Charlene and Bill were obviously very eager to hear what our results were, and I spoke often with them as small pieces of information flowed in from the team.

We knew that Charlene believed the Bull Ring was haunted by the spirit of a man, but we were certain that a majority of the recordings captured were of a female voice.

"I have never seen or heard anything from a woman in this building," she said. "I don't know why a woman would be here."

I explained to her that spirits are not like the living, in that they are not bound by physical limitations. Whoever it was we had captured on tape may not actually have a tie to the building at all; it was possible that this woman was just passing through and chose to interact with us. There really was no way to know for sure at that point.

Interestingly enough, friends of Mike and Jenny Bornstein— the building's previous owners—made a visit shortly after we had conducted our investigation and spoke with Charlene and Bill about some of the odd things the Bornsteins had experienced during their years there. Mike had often seen shadow people in the basement and had it almost completely boarded up. He avoided going down to the lower level of the building as much as he could, and felt very strongly that the basement was haunted.

Charlene spoke to me about another interesting tidbit as well—Mike and Jenny had often talked about a prostitute who may have been killed in the building, which Charlene had never heard of until then. Mr. Bornstein had often seen the apparition of a woman in a red dress, and associated this spectre with the spirit of the unfortunate lady of the night.

"It really made no sense to me that you came in and captured a woman's voice, because I had never heard of anything tragic happening to a woman here," she said. "Do you think it might be her?"

"I can't say one way or another, but it certainly is possible," I replied.

As more and more is uncovered about the ghostly history of the Bull Ring, perhaps information might surface to identify not only those who frequented the building in life, but those who continue to visit from the other side of the veil. One thing is certain—the Bull Ring is haunted. By whom and for what reasons, I do not know, but I look forward to unraveling the mystery one EVP at a time.

Spotlight on Ghosts: Lady of the Lake

As far back as the 1930s, stories have circulated throughout the Dallas area about a spectral woman wandering in search of help. She is reportedly seen by many people near White Rock Lake, though no one knows exactly who she is. One of the most common experiences reported is that of drivers in the area who happen to see a wet and stranded girl near the lake in search of a ride home. Several drivers have stopped to offer the poor girl some assistance, only to have her disappear a short while later, leaving nothing behind but a damp mark in the vehicle where she had been sitting.

This vanishing hitchhiker has fascinated people in the area for decades. Some think she may be the spirit of a young woman involved in some sort of fatal accident on the lake where she and others may have died. Desperate to get home to her family, she provides the driver with an address before suddenly disappearing from the car. Those who have taken it upon themselves to locate the address found that, indeed, the family living there had lost a young woman to a tragedy on the lake.

The ghostly apparition witnessed by many at White Rock Lake may actually be more than one female spirit. Other accounts tell of at least two other women who perished in the water between 1935 and 1942 due to suicide by drowning. Visitors to the area have not only seen the figure of a woman hitchhiking for a ride, but also rising up out of the water before vanishing into thin air.

This legend has survived for nearly a century. Is the lady of the lake still wandering the night asking passersby for help? Could there be several female spirits destined to roam the area for eternity? The only way to find out is to take a drive out to White Rock Lake and see for yourself. You just might end up with an extra passenger . . . or two.

CHAPTER 8

The Majestic Theatre
DALLAS

**Majestic Theatre
exterior
(April Slaughter)**

NO MATTER WHERE YOU LIVE, there is a list of places people "just know" are haunted. Ghosthunting groups discuss them amongst themselves and list the reported phenomena online. A local resident or two can usually tell you all kinds of stories about these places. Some of the ghost stories may be true, while others may be the products of overactive imaginations. Either way, ghostly lore has a way of reaching out to people and drawing them in.

When my husband and I formed The Paranormal Source, we thought a perfect place to start looking for ghosts would be at The Majestic Theatre in downtown Dallas. Any local paranormal group would tell you that they would jump at the chance to investigate this well-known haunt.

The Majestic first opened its doors on April 11, 1921, highlighting performances of entertainers popular during the vaudeville era. Mae West, Bob Hope, and even Harry Houdini were featured there until films became the primary attraction. The Majestic closed after the last showing of the film "Live and Let Die" on July 16, 1973. In 1976, the theatre was donated to the city of Dallas and began undergoing major restoration efforts. When The Majestic re-opened in 1983, it was listed on the National Register of Historic Places and once again provided the community with access to the performing arts.

In the past, management believed that the theatre's benefactor, Karl Hoblitzelle, was still visiting the building even though he had died in 1967. Former actors and actresses were also thought to make their presence known from time to time. The staff reported occasions when all of the phone lines to the theatre would simultaneously light up, but no calls were coming in. Backdrops would often move without having anyone backstage responsible, and odd smells would quickly come and go without any reasonable explanation.

After several attempts to reach those currently on staff at the theatre, I was finally able to speak to the management. Over the past several decades, The Majestic has seen different managers come and go, all having varying opinions on whether or not the historic building was haunted. Sadly, arrangements to investigate the theatre with The Paranormal Source team could not be made, and it seemed that I might never have the chance to walk inside.

Then I received an e-mail one afternoon announcing that my favorite comedian, Eddie Izzard, would be performing at The Majestic as part of his comedy tour. I immediately purchased two tickets to the show. Normally, I would have consulted with my husband to see if we could afford the cost or make the proper arrangements, but this time I figured it would be better for me to ask forgiveness than ask permission. I wanted into The Majestic Theatre—how would I have known that Eddie Izzard would be the one to get me in?

I knew that I would not be able to actually investigate the location, and that hundreds of people would be attending the event, but nothing was going to keep me from asking staff members about the resident ghosts of the theatre while I was there.

Make fun of me if you wish (my husband did), but I was the first person standing at the door, tickets firmly in hand and about a hundred questions in my mind. The large crowd that had accumulated outside the main entrance flooded into the lobby when the doors were finally opened.

The interior of the theatre was truly breathtaking. The elegant staircases and beautiful carved woodwork inside fascinated me. We had to wait for a small time before the doors opened into the main seating area, so I asked Allen to hold our place as I went looking for a staff member to talk to. Every employee I approached was unwilling to discuss paranormal activity with me. I almost gave up on getting any interesting stories until I posed a question to the usher who escorted us to our seats.

"You wouldn't happen to know of any ghost stories related to this place, would you?"

He looked at me a little puzzled. I suppose the question caught him off guard. I was there for a comedy show; why was I asking questions about ghosts?

"Yeah, but I don't think I am supposed to talk about it here," he said.

"That's okay. Here's my card. Call or e-mail me if you'd like sometime later on," I said.

We settled in to watch the show, and laughed when Eddie began to joke about the existence of ghosts.

"If ghosts exist, why are there no goat ghosts?" he asked. He went on to point out that of all the goats that must have been sacrificed in various rituals throughout history, surely some of them would still be around, making ghostly goat sounds.

After the show, I had the chance to ask Eddie whether or not he really believed in ghosts.

"No, I don't," he said. "My mother died when I was six years old and if she were still around, I am sure I would have heard from her by now."

I went home glad to have seen Eddie's show, and also having had the opportunity to see The Majestic for myself, but I was a bit disappointed that I didn't leave with any ghost stories for my notes.

A little over a week passed, and my cell phone rang. I did not recognize the number and almost let the call go to voicemail before I finally decided to answer the call.

"Hello, this is April," I said.

"Hi. I'm calling about The Majestic Theatre in Dallas," said the young man on the line. "A friend of mine gave me your card and said you were interested in hearing about paranormal experiences people have had there."

"Yes! Thank you so much for calling," I exclaimed. "May I ask what your name is?"

"I'd rather not say. I don't want to make anyone upset with me over this."

I agreed to keep his identity anonymous, and then asked him to tell me whatever he could about the haunting of The Majestic.

"I used to work there," he began. "I helped out a lot backstage, and basically did whatever needed to be done. Some of the other employees would say they saw or heard something strange every now and again, but I never really bought into it.

"I remember one evening, after everyone had left following a performance, I was walking down near the orchestra pit and noticed a man still sitting in one of the balcony seats. I thought

I'd make my way up there to see if he needed help or something, but when I got up there, he was gone."

"Did he look like anyone else that might be working there?" I asked.

"I had no idea who he was. He didn't look at all familiar to me. I went back down to the lower level and when I looked up again, the man was still sitting there."

He went on to tell me that he was getting frustrated with the situation, so he asked another employee if she had seen the man as well, which she had not. The premises had been thoroughly checked for anyone who might still be inside before the theatre was locked up for the evening.

"I came back to work not really thinking much about it," he continued. "But other employees would sometimes tell me that they had weird things happen. Someone would hear their name called out when no one was around, or props and things they had put away would somehow make their way back out onto the stage again. Stuff like that."

"Did anything else happen to you after you saw the individual in the balcony?" I asked.

"I never saw the man again, no, but I have to admit I was a little freaked out after that. I always felt like someone was watching me, but who knows if that was just because I was thinking about it too much."

The conversation ended with my thanking him for his call, and asking him if it would be all right to share his story even though he did not want me to share his name. It took some time, but I was finally able to verify that people really did experience things in the theatre that they could not explain.

I wonder if Eddie Izzard had any idea that he had performed in a reportedly haunted theatre when he came to Dallas. Surely there were no "goat ghosts" roaming around the Majestic, but Mr. Hoblitzelle, its creator, might have been there to see the show. He loved this theatre and must be proud to have seen it evolve into what it is today. He may be the lone cause of paranormal happenings within the theatre, or he could be accompanied by performers and guests of the past who find it just too beautiful a place to leave.

Perhaps someday, the theatre will publicly embrace its ghosts. Until then, I will return as a guest enjoying the arts, all the while aware that patrons both seen and unseen are still attracted to the beauty that is The Majestic.

CHAPTER 9

Millermore

DALLAS

Millermore exterior at Dallas Heritage Village
(April Slaughter)

SHORTLY AFTER MOVING TO TEXAS, I began to hear rumors about a mansion on the grounds of the Dallas Heritage Village in Old City Park in Dallas. Several stories were circulating about this historic home that claimed it was host to a variety of unexplained phenomena. Naturally, the stories aroused my curiosity and I wanted to learn more about the house.

Dallas pioneer William Brown Miller and his second wife Minerva originally lived with their family in a modest cabin in Dallas that Mr. Miller had constructed in 1847. The cabin, known as the Miller Log House, now sits close by the Greek Revival style home that the family began working on in 1855 and completed in 1862. For fifteen years, the cabin served as their residence and also one of the first schools of Dallas County. The Miller family and their descendants inhabited the home until 1966, when the last of the Millers passed away. Determined to save the house from destruction, the Dallas County Heritage Society stepped in to preserve its history by carefully dismantling the structure and rebuilding it in the Dallas Heritage Village.

The Miller cabin and Millermore house sit among twenty-five additional historic structures on the property, all moved from their original locations, that now serve as a living history museum.

Our good friend and lead investigator, Jerry Bowers, accompanied Allen and me on a day trip to the village one chilly January afternoon. The sky was heavily overcast and there were fewer than a dozen people wandering the grounds. We took our time and strolled the pathways connecting all of the different buildings, taking pictures along the way. The grounds were so beautifully landscaped and maintained that we could have spent hours exploring all the village had to offer.

Our attention was immediately drawn to Millermore as soon as it came into view. It's a majestic and beautiful home located close to the park's entrance. Several wooden rocking chairs adorn the front porch. A Texas state flag moves with the wind just above the entrance. Unfortunately, on our first trip to the village, the house was not open. Although we were disappointed at not being able to view the interior, we spent some time walking around the house just getting a feel for it.

We walked the remainder of the property, discussing the Millermore and all the ghost stories that have been told about it. We decided that we would return to the village and to the Millermore when it was open to the public.

For as long as the Millermore has been in Dallas Heritage Village, there have been stories of apparitions moving about in almost every area of the house. The figure of a woman, believed to be Mr. Miller's third wife, Emma, has been seen walking from the upstairs master bedroom to the nursery. The odd movement of inexplicable lights on the top floor has also often been reported.

Several paranormal teams have conducted investigations at the Millermore in hopes of capturing the various phenomena, and many believe the ghosts of several children may be playing on the property. EVP recordings captured children's laughter when no children were in or near the home. While I am always a little unnerved when it comes to encountering the ghosts of children, I was pleased to learn that those thought to haunt the Millermore are at least happy and laughing and enjoying themselves.

I wondered whether anyone working in the village had experienced anything paranormal in the house, or any other structure on the property. I contacted staff members to inquire about this very subject.

I was told that no one at the park would confirm or deny paranormal activity in Millermore or anywhere else on the property. Many of the families tied to the buildings and artifacts within the village still live in the area, and it is the staff's job to relay information that is historically accurate and nothing more.

Millermore interior bedroom *(April Slaughter)*

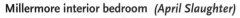

Many paranormal investigation teams have been allowed onto the property to see if they could capture anything anomalous on film, but the village and its staff never participate in the investigations. They believe it is important not to sway their visitors one way or another.

My husband and I cannot resist a good ghost story, and after I had learned about the experiences of others at the Millermore, Allen and I were eager to make a repeat visit. After all, if Emma Miller and the many children who had originally occupied the home were still spiritually linked to it, I definitely wanted to experience them for myself. Just a few short weeks after our initial trip to Dallas Heritage Village, we were back at the house and ready to introduce ourselves to its ghostly inhabitants.

I spoke to a volunteer at the village who has been assisting on the property for over thirteen years; on the day we arrived to walk through the historic home, she was conducting the visitor tour. It was obvious that she thoroughly enjoyed her volunteer time relaying information to guests eager to learn more. At one point during the tour, a young woman asked the volunteer if she believed the home was haunted.

"I've often heard strange noises," she answered. "This is an old house and the floor creaks a lot. I don't know if it is anything paranormal. I just carry about my business and try not to pay too much attention."

I was particularly intrigued when we reached the upstairs level and stood in the large open breezeway running through the center of the house. There are several shadowbox frames showcasing intricately woven human hairpieces hanging on the wall, collected by a family in the Dallas Metroplex. While not historically tied to the house itself, they are beautiful yet eerie, ornate artifacts that made me uneasy. I wasn't sure what they were at first glance, and upon closer inspection I realized that I had never seen anything like them before.

As I stood there staring at the unusual pieces, I felt the distinct sensation of someone brushing my hair away from the back of my neck. Allen hadn't been near me as he was busy wandering around the bedrooms taking pictures, and the remainder of the group had already moved on down the hallway. I stood there doing my best to keep still, hoping the experience would repeat itself, but it didn't. My initial uneasy feeling soon melted away.

The tour guide gathered our group in the hallway where she pointed out a small day bed situated just below a window at the rear of the house. She explained that it was a piece originally owned by William Miller and that he often enjoyed an afternoon nap there, cooled by the breezes that flowed through. When we had first ascended the staircase, the quilt lay neatly atop the bed, as though the bed had just been made. After spending approximately twenty minutes upstairs, we all made our way back to the staircase and past the day bed. I noticed that in the middle of the bed, a slight yet noticeable impression had been made in the quilt as if someone had been sitting on it. I made no mention of it at the time, hoping someone else would point it out and validate my thoughts. But no one else seemed to notice, and we all shuffled back down the stairs to the main floor.

My experiences at the Millermore impressed me, as I had constantly been aware of the movements of the people in the tour group and yet, something unseen had approached me. I believe without a doubt that someone wanted us to notice that they were there. While I didn't have the opportunity to speak to the other visitors individually, I had the sense that they too felt a spiritual presence in the house. They walked through the home with quiet reverence and continually looked backward as if they were expecting to see a spirit from the past walking along behind them.

After the tour came to an end, Allen and I snapped several photos and marveled at the collection of antiques within the home. We made it a point to thank the tour guide for her time as we made our way to the front door to leave.

As we descended the steps of the front porch, I turned around to take another look at the house. I wondered who had touched my hair and if that person had been the same individual who sat on the day bed. I felt a reverence for the history of the house, for the work that went into both building and preserving it, and for the family that may still call it home. For a moment, I thought about the possibility that Emma had been the one to touch my hair as I stood in the upstairs hallway. I wondered if William was anxious for us to finish our tour so that he could take his routine afternoon nap. I don't know who it was for certain, but I do know that I will definitely return to visit the Millermore and the spirits that still reside within it.

CHAPTER 10

The Iris Theatre/ Books & Crannies

TERRELL

**Original marquee for the Iris Theatre
(April Slaughter)**

JUST OVER A YEAR AGO, Allen and I were driving through downtown Terrell when a curious little building caught our attention. You could tell that it had been a fixture on West Moore Avenue for quite some time, and we were both immediately intrigued.

"I wonder if they have any ghosts," said Allen. "Maybe we should stop in sometime and see."

The Iris Theatre originally opened its doors to the public 1925 with "The Lady" as its first feature film. The marquee still sits proudly above the entrance to the building, reading "IRIS" in big letters revamped in red, pink, and green neon. It is turned on every night and hangs above a sign bearing the name of the bookstore you'll find inside today. Books & Crannies is a quaint little bookstore with a lot of charm.

Ron and Gayle Harris own and manage the store, along with two upstairs apartments in the building. Unfortunately, the Iris was ravaged by fire in May 2005, and most of the bookstore was lost in the blaze. The community of Terrell rallied around the couple and donated thousands of books to restock shelves, while several people put in hours of volunteer time to help rebuild and preserve a piece of Terrell's history.

Allen and I set out one Saturday afternoon to visit the bookstore and to introduce ourselves as investigators with The Paranormal Source, Inc. Just as we walked in, we were greeted by a beautiful cat named Maddie, who we learned came to the Iris after becoming an orphan when Hurricane Katrina tore through New Orleans. She has since taken up residence at the bookstore and greets the customers as they come into her home to peruse the large selection of books.

After a quick look around, Allen and I introduced ourselves to Gayle and asked her if she had ever experienced anything paranormal in the building.

"I hear things every now and again," she said. "Sometimes I get the distinct feeling that I am not alone when I know there is no one else in the store with me."

We sat and spoke with Gayle for quite some time before asking her if she would ever be interested in having a professional paranormal investigation team come in and solidify some of her experiences by trying to document activity in the building. She and her best friend "Doc" were excited about the proposition and we scheduled our first of two investigations of the theatre.

One of my major areas of study over the past couple of years has been research on the various "ghost box" devices that are available to investigators in the field. Allen and I have acquired several different versions of radio devices altered to continually scan the radio bands, which in theory provide those on the other side a source of audio noise from which they can form words and sentences to communicate with us. We asked Gayle and her husband if we could experiment with these devices in their bookstore, and they graciously allowed us to try.

One of our first experiments was with a prototype of what is called the MiniBox—a radio device that was inspired by an invention of Colorado resident Frank Sumption. For years, Frank has been building and giving his aptly named "Frank's Boxes" to different researchers for use, but as these are not readily available to the public, Ron Ricketts was inspired to build a version of the device for mass production. I had been given MiniBox Prototype # 3, which we brought along on this particular investigation.

Allen set up the MiniBox in the theatre, as well as our video camera and digital audio recorders to catch whatever information may come through. We all sat in the vintage theatre seats and listened as the sound fluctuated and echoed off the walls. We made small talk as we passed the time, waiting to hear something from the MiniBox.

Suddenly the box blared, "April!" We instantly fell silent and waited. My name had come across the box very clearly, and atop the background radio noise that was continuously moving.

"Hello, is there anyone here with us that would like to make themselves known and say hello?" I asked.

"Yes, several. Active conduit," responded the box.

Just as the box had suddenly begun to communicate, it just as quickly went silent and no other words came through. The radio noise was back to being random and unintelligible, though we waited for quite some time for it to begin again.

When we finally decided to turn the box off and begin working with other equipment, the distinct sound of heavy boots walking across the wood floor startled us. There was no mistaking that sound. Someone unseen had walked into the theatre but could not be glimpsed. When we subsequently reviewed our audio data, we found that the box communication had been clearly captured, but not the sound of the heavy footsteps.

Several times throughout the evening, our investigators reported feeling sudden variations in temperature in different areas of the bookstore. Occasionally, these experiences would be accompanied by slight headaches that would come and quickly dissipate. Lead investigator Jerry Bowers believed he had seen movement near the front register. My first thought was that it could have been the cat moving around, but she had been sitting quietly on the other side of the building when the movement occurred. Everyone in the bookstore was accounted for as well.

As the evening wore on, the team grew tired and we decided it would be best to wrap up and go home. When we prepare for investigations, we are aware that we might be out until the very early morning hours, and while we do all that we can to remain alert, it seems that the activity we encounter can sometimes drain us very quickly despite our best efforts.

After some much-needed rest, we discussed a return visit as a team and arranged another nighttime investigation. Three months later, we were back to see what else we could discover within the nostalgic theatre's walls.

Upon arrival, we split into several small teams to canvass the building. Jerry and I were accompanied by lead investigator Buffy Clary as we entered the theatre's basement, where it was believed a man had fallen down the steep set of stairs and later died from his injuries. In the dark of the basement, we sat in three foldout chairs and began to use the K-II meter to see if we could establish any other presence. Although the lights on the meter would randomly come on, as if someone were approaching the meter, nothing definitive came out of our attempts to obtain answers to our questions. All three of us were quietly talking to one another when we felt a distinct atmospheric change, as if several more people had just walked down the stairs to join us.

After a few minutes, I heard a definite scratching noise on the floor to my right, as if something were being dragged slowly toward me. Jerry and Buffy also reported hearing the same thing, and just as we turned on our flashlights to investigate the source, the sound inexplicably stopped. There were no rodents, bugs, or any other obvious explanation for the noise.

On this occasion, we were especially thrilled to test the arrival of a new ghost box device—Frank's Box #37, which was built and shipped directly to me by Frank Sumption himself. Frank has spent a number of years building and testing his devices, and he gives them to only a handful of people for their research. The old theatre-turned-bookstore would be the first place we used #37 during an official Paranormal Source investigation.

We set up the box in the front of the bookstore in the lounge section, where several of us sat on small couches eager to hear whatever might come through, also keeping in mind that it was possible we might hear nothing at all.

Maddie the cat systematically made her way onto everyone's lap. The box ran uneventfully until I posed a lighthearted question.

"Can you tell me the kitty's name?" I asked.

Almost instantly the box replied with, "Maddie," in what sounded like a young girl's voice.

"Can you tell me your name, please?" I asked, trying to keep the communication going.

"Jan," was the reply, in the same little girl's voice.

While we do not know who Jan was or what her ties were to the theatre, it was clear that she had been speaking to us and that she sounded happy.

The boxes had certainly impressed us as investigators with the amount of direct questions they answered. You never can predict what will come out of the box, if you are fortunate enough to get anything at all. At 2:15 A.M. the next morning, we decided to conclude the investigation and once again head home to rest and discuss the events we had experienced.

The Iris Theatre and its bookstore have a positive energy about them that is definitely inviting, and it is my belief that whoever spiritually visits the old theatre is happy to have people around. Perhaps they are pleased with the fact the theatre, although downsized, still remains to provide a glimpse into a nostalgic past. Maybe the ghostly inhabitants are book lovers, thrilled with the prospect that they can share their literary favorites with others. Whatever the case may be, I was pleased to meet the spirits of the Iris and I am sure they would be more than pleased to meet you.

CHAPTER 11

Catfish Plantation
WAXAHACHIE

Catfish Plantation restaurant exterior (April Slaughter)

IF THERE IS ONE FOOD BESIDES BARBEQUE that Texas is famous for, it would be catfish. I had eaten catfish only a couple of times in my life before moving here, and I hadn't thought it was all that great. The look of shock on my husband's face when I told him that was priceless. I grew up fishing for and eating rainbow trout, straight from the rivers and lakes of Utah, my home state. We didn't eat a lot of catfish in Utah, so Allen made it his mission to introduce me to a proper catfish meal.

As with many other unexpected finds in Texas, I came across the website of the Catfish Plantation restaurant while doing a little searching online. It was relatively close to home, so I thought Allen and I would try dining there one evening. As it turned out, the restaurant was reportedly haunted. Not only would I have the chance to enjoy a good southern catfish meal, I'd be eating it in a haunted restaurant! What more could I ask for?

We made the trip out to Waxahachie with our good friend Jerry Bowers one Saturday afternoon for lunch. The restaurant sits in a residential neighborhood, far removed from the main drag of the town. I immediately fell in love with the place, as it had a humble charm about it.

Ryan Rodriguez—one of the owners of the restaurant—greeted us as we walked in the front door. We chatted for a moment about making the trip over from Dallas for lunch, and I explained to him that Allen and I ran a paranormal investigation team that would love to come in and document activity there sometime. He didn't seem open to the idea at first, as they had already had another team come in just the weekend before, but we soon won him over and we scheduled an investigation of our own.

While we were waiting for our table, I noticed that the restaurant's logo incorporated cartoon-like ghosts, and t-shirts were for sale at the register. On an entry table close by sat a large binder, nearly busting at the seams, with hundreds of personal ghost stories involving restaurant patrons. I took a quick glance through the stories, but did not yet study them because I wanted to investigate the building without knowing too much beforehand about what had happened there.

Allen and I were seated in one of the quaint dining rooms and presented with our menus. After placing our order, we both began pointing out the little intricacies around us as we waited for our meals to arrive. The walls of each dining room were colorfully adorned with different Victorian-style wallpapers, and beautiful pieces of stained glass delicately hung in all of the windows. It felt as if we were sitting in someone's personal dining room rather than in a restaurant, which made us feel welcome and comfortable.

The Catfish Plantation has not always been a restaurant. As might be guessed by its location, the 1895 Victorian was originally a personal residence. It was purchased in 1984 by Tom and Melissa Baker, who remodeled it into a restaurant. Before it was completed and opened to the public, Melissa had several experiences that led her to believe something paranormal may be happening at the Catfish Plantation. For example, a tea urn with cups stacked inside of it had been moved from its proper location on a shelf to the middle of the floor. No one else but Melissa had access to the building. The restaurant's website also describes an instance where Melissa came in to find a freshly brewed pot of coffee waiting for her.

After business was up and running, even the employees began to suspect that someone unseen was vying for their attention as they worked. A fry basket was said to have inexplicably risen in the air and levitated in plain sight for several seconds before crashing to the floor. Food went missing, and various items would be found in locations that didn't make sense. Even the silverware that had been carefully placed at each setting on the tables would be inexplicably crossed over one another or moved into different spots.

It would be a few weeks before my team and I could experience the ghosts of the Catfish Plantation, and it was difficult to remain patient. When the day of our investigation finally came, we met with Ryan and a few guests of his outside on the porch of the restaurant to discuss our plan of action.

After all of our baseline temperature and EMF readings were documented, we set up our video and audio recording equipment, split up into small groups, and began to work on attempting to capture EVP.

While in the kitchen area, Jerry and Allen both heard a female voice call out Allen's name. Had anyone in the restaurant that evening called out to Allen, the rest of the team would have immediately heard it as well, but none of us did.

After about an hour, the entire team convened outside to

discuss what to do next. There wasn't a single person left inside, though we had left our video cameras and digital voice recorders on and in place inside the restaurant. After a few minutes, we heard what sounded like a young female voice.

"Hi," she said. "Come in."

Another few minutes passed, then another unidentified voice—this time male—spoke in a demanding tone.

"Look at me!" he said.

When we all re-entered the restaurant, we decided to conduct a short audio session with the Frank's Box to see if anything interesting would come across. As we passed Allen's video camera, he asked us to all watch out for the tripod so that no one would trip and fall should they snag it with their feet. Much to our surprise, when we watched the video, we heard a disembodied voice speak just before Allen warned us.

"Watch out," was clearly whispered, and in very close proximity to the microphone on the camera. Had someone already known what Allen was going to say?

I honestly did not expect much to come of the Frank's Box session we were about to conduct, but I was pleasantly surprised when it seemed as though someone was trying to communicate with the group.

"John Zaffis," said a male voice, very clearly and with what seemed to be a foreign accent.

John Zaffis is a dear friend of mine who has been working in the paranormal field for over three decades. He is a world-renowned paranormal investigator from Connecticut who has assisted in hundreds of cases, including those involving demonic possession and exorcism. We've worked together on many occasions, and I consider him to be one of the leading experts in the paranormal field.

The Catfish Plantation certainly did not have demons, and whoever was asking for John did so in a lighthearted manner.

It was strange to us that we were in a location that John had never visited, yet someone there knew his name and apparently wanted to speak with him.

"Do you want me to talk to John about this place?" I asked.

"Message," the box responded, and in the same voice that had spoken John's name.

"What is the message?" I asked.

"Love me," said the voice.

It was difficult to discern, but I thought the voice had also said something about John "knowing" something.

"What does he know?" was the next question I posed.

"He knows people," was the response.

And just like that, this man stopped communicating—at least as far as any of us could tell. Short bits and pieces continued to transmit out of the box, but nothing as clear as what had just been spoken. We waited for quite some time before deciding to end the session.

Our group sat there in the dark of the dining room, quietly discussing the night's events. For several minutes, nothing happened. Then something strange caught my attention. Just beyond a set of sliding doors that separate two of the dining rooms, I watched as a short, shadowy figure quickly floated through the adjacent room close to the floor. At first, I thought it might have been the result of a car driving by. I said nothing, and kept watching, aware of anything moving on the road outside. It was late and no cars were passing by. I saw the figure twice more within the next couple of minutes, moving along the same path and direction it had taken the first time.

By early morning, the team was exhausted and ready to pack it up and head home. All in all, our visit to the Catfish Plantation had been an interesting experience, and we agreed that possibly several different entities were commonly seen, felt, and heard there.

We had not been the first paranormal team to conduct an investigation of the Catfish Plantation, and we would certainly not be the last. Not only was I able to interact with the ghosts of the restaurant, but I was able to enjoy the absolute best catfish meal I had ever eaten. So, whether you visit for a good meal or a good scare, the experiences you will discover at the Catfish Plantation are simply to die for.

West Texas

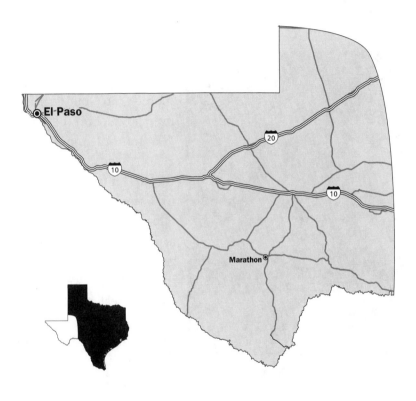

El Paso
Plaza Theatre

Marathon
Gage Hotel

Plaza Theatre
EL PASO

Entrance facade of the Plaza Theatre
(Sheri Smith)

WHEN I WAS IN junior high school, my mother took me to see a live production of "The Phantom of the Opera" at our local downtown theatre. It would be the first time I ever had the opportunity to visit such a place and to see such a grand performance. I sat in complete awe in my balcony seat and watched the amazing story unfold in front of me. I had never seen anything so wonderful in all of my life, and I not only fell in love with the story of the Phantom, but also with the theatre in which I had seen it.

When the performance ended and the patrons began shuffling out, I asked my mother if I could stay for just a bit longer to watch the theatre crew below work on breaking down the set on stage. They worked quickly, and soon everything was prepared to start the show all over again the next evening. Just as my mother and I were about to leave, I noticed a stagehand as he walked out onto the platform with what looked like a lamp without a shade. He set it down in front of the large curtain and switched on the light. Almost every other light in the theatre immediately went dark.

I noticed an usher walking through the empty rows of seats, gathering up trash.

"Excuse me sir, why is that light put on the stage?" I asked.

"That's the ghost light," he said. "They put that up there every night before the theatre closes to keep the resident ghosts from messing with the sets."

As I grew older, I noticed that almost every major theatre house I visited engaged in this same tradition. They all had various explanations for leaving on the ghost light, but the belief that they actually had ghosts in every one of the theatres was universal. Surely they couldn't *all* be haunted, but I was intrigued by the idea nonetheless.

Over the past few years since I moved to Texas, I have researched my fair share of haunted locations in the state. I often think of the ghost light from all those years ago, and was curious as to whether or not Texas had any haunted theatres of its own.

My initial exposure to the Plaza Theatre had nothing to do with ghosts. Allen and I had been in El Paso for a quick visit with friends when we were invited to accompany them to a film festival being hosted at the Plaza.

Jokingly, the first question I presented to our friends was, "Is it haunted?"

Their response was that yes, the theatre had ghosts—many of them, in fact. I had been excited for the evening beforehand, but now I couldn't wait to get there.

When the Plaza first opened its doors to the public on September 12, 1930, it was the largest theatre in the United States located between Dallas and Los Angeles. The façade resembled that of a Spanish Mission and the interior was highly elaborate.

While most other businesses were struggling with the onslaught of the Depression in the 1930s, the Plaza Theatre's patronage flourished and continued to entertain the public until a steep decline in the 1950s. The arrival of drive-in movie theatres and television presented an economic challenge, and the Plaza was eventually sold in the early 1970s.

The Plaza's demolition seemed imminent in 1986, until the surrounding El Paso community rallied to raise the $1 million dollars required to save it. Four short years later, the theatre was donated to the city, which has since poured a great amount of time and money into restoring the historic site.

When our small group arrived at the theatre, we took our seats in the performance hall, which is made to look like a Spanish hacienda, complete with windows, greenery, and a beautifully painted starry night sky. What a feast for the eyes! Even while watching the film we had come to the theatre to see, I often caught myself looking around at the lavishly detailed interior.

I silently wondered who, if anyone, was haunting the Plaza Theatre, and if I would be able to find any documentation to support the rumor. A few days later, after returning home from our road trip, Allen and I began doing a little research online and found that there were several different stories that had evolved over the years since the theatre first opened.

One of the most popular stories is that the ghost of a young bride refuses to leave the site, as the theatre now stands in the very spot where her home once stood and, unfortunately, where she lost her life. Her husband, a high-ranking Spanish official, was an extremely jealous man who kept his bride isolated for fear she would be unfaithful in the event that other prospective suitors came calling. His jealousy would ultimately consume him. He returned home to his bride one evening, angrily accusing the young woman of infidelity before strangling her to death. In an attempt to cover up the crime, he set the home ablaze before riding off under the cover of night.

The apparition of a woman seen in the theatre is thought to be the ghost of this young woman. Despite having met such a grisly end, she seems content to water the plants in the theatre (although they aren't real), as she might have watered flowers in her own garden during happier days. I wonder what became of her murderous husband.

It seems the most common phenomenon within the theatre is the sighting of several apparitions, by both patrons and theatre employees alike. A young man dressed to the hilt in a military uniform is often seen lighting and smoking a cigarette near the entrance to the balcony. Smoking is not permitted anywhere in the theatre, and when individuals have approached the soldier to kindly ask him to extinguish his cigarette, he quickly disappears before they reach him. The smell of cigarette smoke lingers in the air long after the soldier vanishes, as if he continues to smoke but has decided it is best to do so unseen.

I spoke with one former employee of the theatre who asked to remain anonymous. He admitted that he avoided going into the basement area because he felt immediately uneasy and unwelcome as soon as he entered.

"I don't get spooked very easily," he said. "But that basement was not a fun place to be. It always felt like someone was right on my heels the entire time I was down there. I never saw anything, but I could have sworn I heard something like a dog growling a couple of times—like how a really hostile animal would sound."

Paranormal investigators have frequently visited the Plaza Theatre hoping to catch the reported activity on tape. While some of them report that nothing out of the ordinary has occurred during their time there, others will tell you that the building is one of the most active they have investigated to date.

Researching the paranormal can often require a great deal

of patience. I know from experience that ghosts and spirits do not always make themselves known on our time table. In my opinion, making repeat visits to a location, even at varying times of the day or night, can often verify legitimate activity, or debunk it all together. Unless you are dealing with a residual type of phenomenon, you really cannot predict when something paranormal is about to occur. Most of the time, it is all up to luck.

I know people are often disappointed when they expect a lot to happen and they end up with little or no results on their first try. Don't give up! Just as we the living have the ability to govern our actions, so do the dead. Establishing trust can often be a big part of the equation!

Those eager to witness a paranormal event can sometimes resort to provocation to try and "stir up" activity. I've seen these methods work, but I have also seen them backfire. Provoking anything in a negative or combative tone is not likely to elicit a positive response, and you may not be aptly prepared for the reaction you might receive. In my experience, you attract the energy you put out. The paranormal does not need to be frightening, though a good scare isn't always a bad thing either! The element of surprise is what attracts us all.

Our lives are so busy that I think a lot of the activity around us goes largely unnoticed until we take the time to slow down and focus on it. Have you ever thought you saw someone out of the corner of your eye, only to turn and realize that nobody was there? What about those nights you've heard your name called out just before you fell asleep? Oftentimes, we chalk these things up to our imaginations and convince ourselves it is all in our heads. What if it isn't?

The ghostly apparitions witnessed within the walls of the Plaza Theatre were not seen when someone was looking for them. Instead, they chose to show themselves to ordinary people just going about their business or treating themselves to a little entertainment. Who they are and why they are tied to the theatre itself is largely unknown, but as with most every major theatre, the staff of the Plaza honor their resident spirits by leaving their own ghost light lit on stage after every performance.

Spotlight on Ghosts: El Muerto—The Headless Horseman of West Texas

We're all familiar with the legend of Sleepy Hollow and the terrifying headless horseman who stalked the local community in the story, but did you know that Texas has a headless horseman of its own? The legend of El Muerto, or the "Dead One," stretches back to the days of cattle rustlers and outlaws, dirt trails and cowboy fights. While some believe him to be merely a product of myth, there are those who claim he might have actually existed.

In 1850, one of the most famous of all Texas Rangers—Bigfoot Wallace—allegedly captured a Mexican outlaw simply known as Vidal, who had been raiding ranches and stealing cattle and horses. Texas Rangers had long been working to keep the incidents of theft at a minimum, but outlaws continued to sweep across the south. Rangers had done everything they could to send a clear message to other outlaws that the thievery would not be tolerated, but their efforts had been largely unsuccessful.

Bigfoot Wallace reportedly executed Vidal upon his capture, tied his decapitated head and sombrero to the saddle horn of a wild mustang, secured his body in the animal's saddle, and sent the horse out to roam the plains. Cowboys began to see the horse and its unfortunate rider aimlessly riding through the hills and became so afraid that they shot at it with their guns. Over time, El Muerto became an omen of bad things to come and was credited in stories of the misfortunes of others. Once the horse had been cornered in present-day Uvalde, Texas, the body of the one-time rustler was finally laid to rest. This, however, would not be the last time El Muerto was seen. Stories began to spread like wildfire that he was still riding in the hills and among the ranches he had once stolen from.

The legend of the headless horseman of Texas is still alive and well today, as many ranchers and travelers throughout west Texas have reported seeing the ghostly apparition on clear and moonlit evenings; a large and foreboding presence, seemingly destined to an eternity of riding headless through the plains on a wild mustang.

CHAPTER 13

Gage Hotel
MARATHON

Gage Hotel exterior
(© focalplane.com)

ONE OF THE THINGS I LOVE most about my husband is his willingness to just pick up and go with me to random places I want to visit. It is not at all uncommon for me to discover information online about some obscure place in Texas, and ask Allen on a whim to take me there; not tomorrow, not next week, but right that second. I am blessed to have a husband who enjoys going on little adventures, especially paranormal ones.

Marathon, Texas, is not exactly a major tourist destination. It is far removed from the big sprawling metropolises like Dallas, Houston, and Austin. It is nestled in the wide open frontier of west Texas, near the north entrance of the Big Bend National Park.

"Honey, I want you to take me to Marathon," I said to Allen.

"You want to run a marathon? Since when?" he teased me.

"I want to see the Gage Hotel," I said. "I hear they have a fantastic restaurant."

"It's a little far to travel to Marathon just for a meal, hon."

"They have ghosts, Allen."

"When are we leaving?" he asked.

Within an hour or so after that conversation, Allen and I were in the car and on our way from Dallas to west Texas. I knew that the hotel had a restaurant in-house, as I had perused the menu online just a day or so before. Luckily, we had an entire weekend to make the trek out and enjoy ourselves. The drive was nearly nine hours each way, so heading to the Gage Hotel for dinner after work one night during the week was definitely not an option.

After we had been on the road for a few hours, the scenery became bleak, so I thought I would read a little more about the Gage Hotel online. Thanks to our modern-day ability to access information on-the-go, I was quickly able to locate the hotel's website on my cell phone.

Businessman Alfred Gage moved from Vermont to Texas in 1927 and acquired 500,000 acres to operate a ranch. The Gage Hotel was originally built as headquarters for the ranch, but Mr. Gage was only able to enjoy it for one year before his death in 1928.

J.P. Bryan and his wife Mary Jon purchased the building in 1978 for $30,000 and spent nearly twenty years pouring their time and money into making the Gage Hotel the beautiful reality it is today.

The closer we got to Marathon, the more desolate things began to look. I've been through some pretty sparse-looking terrain before, but west Texas definitely takes the cake. I grew up in Utah where there were all sorts of places to roam around and discover, including deserts and such, but I am much more of a mountain girl. I like hills and trees, lakes and rivers; all of those things seemed fairly far off in the distance out here.

We reached Marathon at about 5:00 P.M. that evening, and we drove around a bit to get a feel for the area. I chuckled when

I saw a tumbleweed dance across the street. It felt genuinely "old west" to me.

"Want to move to west Texas?" asked Allen.

I shot him a look, and without having said a word he knew what I was thinking.

"We'll stay put, then," he said.

"I don't mind visiting. In fact, I think it's quite fun to find places like this," I said. "Life gets so busy and we're always so wrapped up in technology and whatnot. Out here, that stuff isn't so important. It's kind of nice to be somewhere that doesn't make you feel so rushed."

"So, can we leave your phone in the car when we go in for dinner?" he asked.

"What? Are you crazy? No."

A big grin stretched across his face, as if he'd made a point in asking about the phone. I suppose he had, but I did my best to ignore it.

We pulled up to the Gage Hotel and I was instantly taken with the place. The landscaping was pristine, and I particularly enjoyed the letters spelling out the name of the hotel on the roof of the building. We walked inside, and I approached a lady working at the front desk.

"Are you here to check in?" she asked.

"No, actually, we're just here to have dinner," I said. "But would you mind if I asked you a couple of questions about the hotel first?"

"Please do. What can I help you with?"

"I've done a lot of reading up on the Gage Hotel lately, and a lot of people claim the hotel is haunted. Is that true?" I asked.

"We have a couple of friendly ghosts here, yes," she replied.

An older gentleman had overheard my conversation with the woman at the desk and tapped me on the shoulder.

"Excuse me ma'am, I just thought I would tell you that I

know there are ghosts in this hotel," he said.

I introduced myself and shook the gentleman's hand. I didn't think to ask his name (which I regret now), but I remember thinking to myself that he looked an awful lot like my late grandfather. He was chewing on a toothpick, which is something my grandfather always did. He asked me if I had a minute to hear his story, which I most certainly did.

"My wife and I come to drive through Big Bend every year, and we stay at least one night every time," he continued. "One evening, my wife excused herself to the lady's room just after we had checked in, and as I was opening my overnight bag on the bed, I realized I had left my wallet at the front desk.

"When I came back to the room, my wife was just coming out of the restroom and everything that had been in my overnight bag was neatly stacked outside of it on the bed. I asked my wife if she had unpacked the bag, but she hadn't come out from the restroom until I came back from retrieving my wallet."

"Do you remember what room you were in?" I asked.

"No, that was several years ago. Not sure which one of them it was now," he replied.

"Did anything else odd occur that night?"

"Yes. My wife and I go to bed fairly early, so we were already asleep by nine o'clock or so that night. At just after two in the morning, I woke up thinking I heard someone's radio going off in another room because I heard someone softly singing. I sat up in bed, and nudged my wife."

The gentleman told me that he and his wife sat for several minutes and listened to someone signing. The strange thing was, they realized it was not coming from a radio, rather from somewhere in their own room! The voice was muffled, and they didn't understand the words or know the song, but he said that he and his wife were not able to fall asleep again for quite some time after that incident.

The gentleman's wife approached him and indicated it was time for them to leave. I thanked him for taking the time to tell me his story, and bid him and his wife a good evening.

Just as the restaurant opened at six o'clock, Allen and I were seated for dinner in the hotel's Café Cenizo. Allen enjoyed the Bison Rib Eye and I the Sautéed Shrimp. While the meal was not inexpensive, it was certainly delicious and well worth the drive all on its own to experience.

The drive back home was a long one, and we didn't get in until nearly three o'clock the next morning, but we had enjoyed our impromptu trip to the historic Gage Hotel. When we finally rolled out of bed at close to noon, I went right to my computer with my mandatory cup of coffee to look up more of the ghostly lore associated with the hotel.

Over the course of the next couple of weeks, I exchanged e-mails with various hotel staff about the paranormal activity they have experienced. None of them wished to be named, but they offered several stories of encounters with the unknown inside the hotel.

One woman who has worked at the Gage Hotel for thirteen years told me about an apparition seen in the hotel in the middle of a slow business day.

"It was about five years ago, and I remember that we only had one room booked out for that day," she said. "I was in the basement when a couple of children came down to ask me who the lady upstairs was. I told them that there was no one else in the hotel at the time, so I wasn't sure who they were talking about.

"They told me that she had long hair and she was wearing a floor-length dress. She had patted them both on their heads, but said nothing to them. The children told me that they watched as she went in and out of several of the guest rooms. I went upstairs to look around, but I found no one else there."

I asked if she had any idea who the woman may have been, but she did not.

"One of my night auditors also mentioned to me that he believed he had a visitor on some of the evenings he was working," she continued. "One of the leather chairs would make the sound like someone had just sat down in it, and he could even see an indention in the cushion as if someone were really sitting there."

Several past guests of the Gage Hotel have reported that just after dark, partial and full-body apparitions are seen in the hallways and out on the patio. Personal items are often moved from one area to another while guests are sleeping, but beyond that minor inconvenience, the guests have never complained.

Perhaps on some lazy Saturday in the future, Allen and I will once again make the journey out through the west Texas plains to stay an evening at the Gage Hotel. I've done my research and I already know that when I get there, I'm going to personally request a night in room #10.

Spotlight on Ghosts: Marfa Lights

In the 1950s, reports of a strange phenomenon occurring in Presidio County began to attract a lot of attention. Strange balls of various-colored light appeared at night—sometimes moving erratically or hovering completely still in the air. Witnesses have often reported that these balls of light appear in pairs or even larger numbers and can be seen ranging from a matter of seconds to hours before finally disappearing.

The Marfa Lights, also known as the Marfa Ghost Lights, have never appeared in the daytime and seem to be a strictly nocturnal phenomenon. No clear explanation has ever been provided, but many believe the lights to be a manifestation of spirit activity and contend that they are indeed a paranormal occurrence. Skeptics often attribute the phenomenon to passing vehicles or lights from nearby homesteads or changes in atmospheric conditions, but the strange and unpredictable pattern of movements make it difficult to say one way or another.

The lights appear randomly in the nighttime hours, and occur year-round. They are not easily approached, however, as they appear above private property. They are often seen at varying distances and have been captured over the years in both still photography and video footage. Some visitors contend that upon witnessing the Marfa Lights, they have had profoundly personal spiritual experiences and do not believe they should simply be dismissed as a scientific mystery.

Whatever the explanation may be behind the Marfa Lights, they continue to attract curious onlookers and visitors from all over the state of Texas. A fascinating display of color and movement, the Marfa Lights may indeed be something purely environmental, but what if they're not? Perhaps the ghosts of Presidio County often gather together in an attempt to make themselves known in the late-night hours. We may not ever know what the lights truly are, but as long as they continue to appear we are sure to be continually mystified by them.

Central Texas

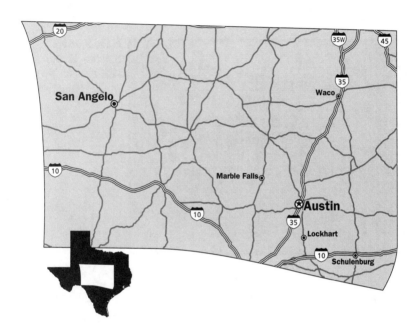

Austin
Driskill Hotel

Lockhart
Caldwell County Jail Museum

Marble Falls
Dead Man's Hole

San Angelo
Old Fort Concho

Schulenburg
Von Minden Hotel

Waco
Oakwood Cemetery

CHAPTER 14

Old Fort Concho
SAN ANGELO

**Headquarters
building at Old
Fort Concho
*(April Slaughter)***

WHAT IS MY DREAM as a paranormal investigator? What
am I really looking for? Is it all about stalking around in the
dark with my digital voice recorder and camera, hoping to have
something unseen scare me out of my wits? No. Honestly, I am
frightened by very little when I am ghosthunting. Crazy things
can and do happen, but when it comes right down to it, I am far
more afraid of the living than I am of the dead. Ghosts aren't
going to mug me or steal my car. They aren't going to be talking
on their cell phones in traffic and cause a major accident. Those
of us who have a pulse seem to cause far more trouble than
those who don't.

My dream is that one day, as time and our understanding
of the paranormal progresses, we will be able to have real-time,
two-way conversations with those on the other side without having so many obstacles to overcome. Imagine all of the mysteries

we could solve—the knowledge we could gain about life after death! Until that day comes, I'll keep diving in head-first with the knowledge I *do* have and sharing what I know with anyone who wants to hear it.

If I could suggest any one type of location for new ghost-hunters looking for practice, it would definitely be historic forts. Why? Well, forts are usually spacious with a mix of buildings and open space. They are often well preserved and contain living quarters, hospitals, working areas, and even cemeteries—all places where a lot of human emotion and experiences can imprint on the environment. Of course, not all forts are haunted, but if you can find one with a reputation for being paranormally active, it might be a fantastic place to start.

One such place in Texas is Fort Concho. If you do a little searching online, you will find all sorts of stories about the fort and theories as to who might be haunting it. I hadn't known that ghosts resided on the fort property at the time of my first visit, but I would come to hear stories of them as my research for this project began. It has been two years now since I was introduced to Fort Concho, but the afternoon I spent there left such an impression on me that when the opportunity to write *Ghosthunting Texas* presented itself, I had to make sure this particular fort was included.

One of Allen's high school friends had moved out to San Angelo from east Texas, and on our way out for a visit one summer afternoon, Allen suggested we stop in at Fort Concho to have a look around.

"We've got a little time to kill. Let's walk around and see what the place is like," he said.

The fort was originally established in 1867 as a small collection of tents where the Middle and North Concho rivers met. Soldiers patrolled and kept the peace in west Texas, protected settlements, and mapped out the expansive frontier. The fort's boundaries stretched over sixteen hundred acres of land, but in 1889 it was abandoned. In 1961, Fort Concho was deemed a National Historic Landmark. Today it stands as one of the most beautifully preserved forts in the state. Twenty-four buildings remain on the property, seventeen of them original, and all of them restored and well maintained by the city of San Angelo.

Looking back on my initial visit, I wish I would have stopped and asked someone at the fort if it had a haunted reputation. Many forts do, but it hadn't really crossed my mind at the time. Allen and I spent an hour or so walking around and enjoying the grounds. I was particularly enthralled with the E.H. Danner Museum of Telephony, where several models of telephones from the past to the present were displayed. I remember commenting to Allen that if we could come that far in communicating with each other as living, breathing human beings, certainly we had hope of establishing a better connection with those on the "other side" someday.

Little did I know that a couple of years later, I'd be researching Fort Concho for a book about Texas haunts. The story that I first ran across was that of a little girl named Edith Claire Grierson, the daughter of Colonel Benjamin Grierson. He had been post commander and lived in Officers Quarter's #1 (also referred to as OQ1) with his family. In 1878, at the age of thirteen, Edith became seriously ill with typhoid fever and died after thirteen agony-filled days. Apparently, she wasn't ready to leave the house even then.

Sometime in the early part of the 1990s, B.D. Shaffer, a delivery driver assisting local florist Tom Ridgway, arrived at Fort Concho to help deliver flowers following a funeral. As B.D. entered Officer's Quarters # 1 (the former Grierson residence), he was asked to place one bouquet in two of the upstairs bedrooms while Tom continued to work downstairs. B.D. placed one arrangement in the west bedroom and walked across the hall to the east bedroom to place the other. He had lost his right eye in a previous accident, which helped him to develop excellent peripheral vision in his left eye. As he entered the second bedroom, he noticed a young girl sitting on the floor to his left. After putting the flowers on the dresser, he turned toward the girl, but she suddenly disappeared from sight.

When B.D. returned to the fort for their Christmas program the following December, a docent working in OQ1 approached him and they began talking about the house. After B.D. told her about his experience with the little girl in the bedroom upstairs, the docent escorted him into another room to show him a picture of Edith Grierson. The girl he had seen months earlier was the same girl in the picture.

That incident was not the only one where someone encountered the little girl's ghost. In June 2003, the new assistant city manager for San Angelo, Harold Dominguez, and his family stayed in OQ1 as they waited for their permanent home to become available.

As reported by Perry Flippin in an August 2003 article published in the *San Angelo Standard Times*, Harold's wife, Andrea, had come face-to-face with the specter of a little girl in OQ1. She had been busy gathering and packing the family's things when she looked up and saw a young girl about the age of twelve descending the staircase. She was wearing a long, peach-colored dress and had long brown hair pulled back from her face. They stared at each other for a brief moment before the girl's image disappeared. Neither Andrea nor her husband, Harold, had known about the history of OQ1 or that a girl matching the description Andrea provided had passed away in the house.

Not being a big believer in the paranormal, Andrea convinced herself that it must have been a trick of the eye, or an optical illusion produced by the afternoon sun as it shone through one of the home's windows. It hadn't happened in the middle of the night, rather late in the afternoon, and so she made no mention of it to her husband until he asked her if she had experienced anything strange during their stay.

As they discussed it further, more and more strange occurrences seemed to stand out in their minds. A desk chair had been moved out of its position, and neither of them had moved it. As the couple slept one evening, both were awakened at close to midnight by the sound of a loud female voice wailing just outside the bedroom window. After just four days in OQ1, the Dominguez family decided to relocate to a motel. When Mr. Flippin presented a picture of Edith Grierson to the couple, Andrea indicated that she looked like the young girl she had seen on the staircase.

Other visitors to OQ1 have often reported feeling dramatic drops in temperature throughout various areas of the house, and attribute it to Edith's presence trying to manifest. Even on a warm day when the air outside is still, people feel these cold spots moving around the house.

Visitor and Volunteer Services Coordinator Cory Robinson has worked at the fort for nearly nine years. When I spoke with him, I asked about the various reports of paranormal activity, and whether or not he had personally experienced anything of note.

"Sometimes when I've been inside Barracks #5, I have heard what sounds like heavy footsteps hitting the wooden porch," he said. "If you are familiar with large, heavy leather boots with those thick soles, you know that they have a very distinct sound when someone takes a step in them. This wasn't at all like the shuffling sound of a visitor's tennis shoes. I have heard the sound of those footsteps on more than one occasion."

"Is there any specific time you experience the sound of these footsteps?" I asked him.

"It only seems to happen when stormy weather is moving

in. Beyond that, no—there is nothing else I can think of that ties the incidents together."

As Fort Concho prepared for a Christmas program one year, Cory stayed the night in OQ1. He knew about the building's reputation, but didn't think much about it.

"The day of the program, I got up and got into the shower," Cory said. "While I was in the bathroom, someone or something slammed the door shut. It wasn't hard enough to shake anything, but forceful enough to make me hear it over the water running."

Cory never discovered an explanation.

I have not yet had the opportunity to introduce myself to Edith or to any of the other spirits that may be roaming the grounds of Fort Concho, but I do know that I will be back to try. They might be the souls of those once dedicated to the service of their country, their family members, or simply those passing through. In any case, the ghosts of Fort Concho's past seem very much a part of its present, and quite possibly its future.

CHAPTER 15

Oakwood Cemetery
WACO

Coke and Wallace
grave markers at
Oakwood Cemetery
(April Slaughter)

IF YOU TAKE THREE OF MY FAVORITE THINGS—
cemeteries, ghost stories, and thunderstorms—and roll them
all together into one experience, you'd have my definition of a
perfect day. You already know by now that wandering around
cemeteries is a favorite pastime of mine, and that ghost stories
are a huge part of my everyday life, but did you also know that I
would take a stormy day over a sunny one anytime of the year?
It's easy to enjoy a sunny and warm afternoon; they are uneventful and calm. It is the chaos of a storm that attracts me. I revel
in the constant push and pull of the environment and its unpre-
dictability. I am the person out in the wind recording the crazy
conditions on camera, rather than taking the safe route and
waiting it out indoors.

Most people hide themselves away from the rain, lightning,
and thunder. I want to wander around and read headstones as a

storm rolls on above me, and the Oakwood Cemetery in Waco provided me with the perfect opportunity to do so. The day I made my first visit, I had not planned it to coincide with a thunderstorm, but it pleased me a great deal that it happened to work out that way.

Allen and I arrived mid-morning on a stormy spring day. The softened, rain-soaked earth gave a little every time we took a step. The air was warm and thick with humidity that stuck to our skin like sweat after a hard run. I wasn't going to complain. I had heard many a ghost story about this place, and I was hoping I would be able to add my own to the mix.

Land that was once used as a race track and fairgrounds became the Oakwood Cemetery in 1898. Individuals originally interred in other cemeteries in Waco were relocated to Oakwood that year, as the grounds were far better maintained and provided a more pleasant setting for their final resting places. The burial grounds stretch 157 acres, and by April 1969 there were nearly nineteen thousand graves. Today, almost thirty-five thousand souls are buried within the Oakwood Cemetery.

As Allen and I wandered aimlessly through the scattered headstones, two in particular caught my attention. Atop large stone pillars stood the carved figures of two men, each facing one another. I wanted to photograph them, as I had never seen anything like that before. As I approached the markers, the rain suddenly began to pour down. As stubborn as I am, I decided it was worth the risk of getting muddy to get a picture.

Allen had turned on one of our digital recorders, despite the sound of thunder and rain. After taking a few photographs, I looked at my shoes to find that they were indeed covered in mud and grass.

"I think I had better find a mud puddle to wash off my shoes," I said, not realizing that I had made the wrong reference.

Immediately following my statement on the recorder, a male voice corrects me.

"With water!" he said.

At the time of the recording, I was standing between the statues of the two men, whom I would later find out were not only Texas historical figures, but best friends who wanted to be just as close in death as they were in life—Richard Coke, a former governor who died in 1897, and Dr. David Wallace, a psychiatric pioneer who died in 1911.

Were either of these two men the one I heard correcting me when I played back the recording? I can't be sure, but I wouldn't be the first to experience something unexplained in that very spot between these two elaborate headstones. Several locals reported to me that they often spent time here and had also recorded a disembodied voice speaking to them. The voice often pokes fun and, at times, can even be heard laughing. Whoever he is, he seems pleased with his surroundings and enjoys it when those of us still living pass by for a visit.

Being able to see the likeness of a person, or an actual photograph incorporated into their memorials makes a cemetery experience more human to me. I feel as though it puts me in touch with who the person was when they were alive, and knowing even just a small part of their story establishes a sort of connection, however slight and fleeting it may be.

When it is my time to go, I do not want to be forgotten amidst a collection of stones. Would someone want to know who I was, or what impact I made on the world? Whoever is given the responsibility of laying me to rest when my time comes, I can only hope they will see it fitting to remember me with a unique stone or carving. If not, chances are I won't stay quiet about it for long!

Oakwood Cemetery is filled with all kinds of different headstones and markers. As we walked through just a few of the acres that sprawled out in front of us, Allen and I saw and photographed some of the most beautiful statues I had ever seen in a graveyard. Life-sized angels were scattered all around, each with their own individual style of grace and beauty.

"Hey, look at this headstone, April," said Allen. "It looks like it's been shot at."

"What? Why would anyone shoot at a headstone?" I asked, puzzled.

"I'm guessing, and I could be completely wrong here, that someone had it in for this guy," he said.

The headstone he was referring to belonged to a man named William Cowper Brann, a Waco journalist who, at the time of his death in 1898, owned and edited the *Iconoclast* newspaper—a controversial publication in which he fervently attacked groups such as African-Americans, Baptists, Episcopalians, and the British. He often wrote about his distaste for Baylor University, which he claimed was involved in importing children from South America to place in the administration's homes as servants. He was also very outspoken about Baylor being corrupted by sexual misconduct, and warned that any parents who enrolled their daughters there were taking the risk that they would be raped.

Brann's statements had upset many people in the community, and would ultimately lead to his demise. Tom Davis, a local man whose daughter attended Baylor, was highly insulted by Brann's attacks on the university and took it upon himself to shoot him. The bullet entered Brann's left lung and exited through his chest, but he was able to turn and shoot Davis several times, leaving him to die in the doorway of a local cigar shop. Brann lived until the next morning before dying in his home.

Below the word "TRUTH" spelled out on the headstone is a profile view of Brann's face, with a bullet hole in the temple. Locals say this bullet hole turned up on the stone only after

Brann had been buried in Oakwood Cemetery. Apparently, some Waco residents were still adamantly opposed to Brann and his writings even though he was already dead.

Individuals I spoke to after visiting the cemetery believe an apparition that appears near Brann's grave may indeed be him, but also say that his appearances are erratic and do not last for more than a few seconds. Those who have seen his picture say the apparition bears a striking resemblance to the man, and wonder if this once-impassioned writer is haunting Oakwood Cemetery to make sure he and his ideas are never forgotten.

Angel memorial at Oakwood Cemetery
(April Slaughter)

Perhaps he is restless because the living are still taking their "shots" at him and his infamous newspaper.

Oakwood Cemetery has become a favorite of ghosthunters over the years due to its reputation for providing incredible EVP evidence and the occasional sighting of ghostly specters. It is a landscape of eclectic style and beauty, and a testament to the human desire to honor those who have been laid to rest.

I've been through my share of cemeteries, but this one impressed upon me a great sense of peace. I walked, read names and dates, and took dozens of pictures. I ended up a soaking wet mess from the rain as a result, but I would do it again in a heartbeat. I could have spent all day wandering about, and probably will on the next chance I have to make the trip back out to Waco. Hopefully, another storm will blow in and make it an equally perfect day.

I'll always wonder who it was that reminded me that water would be a better solution for me to clean my shoes with than mud, and if they're always so willing to be heard. Should you ever have the chance to visit Oakwood Cemetery, remember—tread lightly as you walk through, for you just never know who might be walking right alongside you.

Spotlight on Ghosts: The Devil's Backbone

The Texas Hill Country is home to forty-seven hundred acres of beautiful landscapes and Native American history. The Indians revere this area as sacred land, and taking a drive through it is sure to convince any visitor that it is just that. The Indians, however, aren't the only ones who believe the Devil's Backbone is a unique place. It has earned a reputation for unexplained phenomena in nearly every form and continues to draw visitors not only in search of beautiful country to see and explore, but also those seeking paranormal encounters.

Legend has it that the apparitions of Native Americans are often seen by hunters and hikers exploring the many trails that wind in and out of the Devil's Backbone country. Moving slowly through the trees, they have reportedly been seen following closely behind those alone in the hills.

Campers have told many stories about witnessing an entire troop of mounted Confederate cavalry suddenly appearing in front of them and then quickly disappearing. One story in particular tells of a group of men who experienced the sound of pounding hooves rushing toward their cabin. The incident prompted them to inspect the area outside the cabin, but they found no physical evidence that horses had even been close by.

Apparitions have become so commonplace that locals have come to expect them rather than be surprised by them. Ghostly cattle ranchers driving their herds through the hills are just another example of the type of encounters people continue to report today. Even the ghosts of monks are often seen. What keeps these spirits tied to the hills may never be discovered, but chances are that anyone willing to brave the dark just might have a tale or two of their own to share when the sun rises the next morning, as a night in the Devil's Backbone could be a very long night.

CHAPTER 16

Dead Man's Hole
MARBLE FALLS

Boulder-lined
entrance to
Dead Man's
Hole
(April Slaughter)

PARANORMAL PHENOMENA can pop up anywhere. Creepy old buildings and so-called "ghost towns" are not the only places one might be able to find and interact with the spirits of those who have crossed over. Fact is, you can't judge a location simply on how it looks. Some of the scariest places I have ever been were not at all the kind that people would normally think of as haunted. Have I encountered ghosts in dilapidated old homes and buildings? Absolutely! I have also seen my fair share of phenomena in pristine, newly built structures and entirely unassuming locations. Sites in the great outdoors have often proven to be some of the most interesting and fun to visit and investigate. I think it is important to keep in mind that anywhere you might go, someone else has been there before you—and still might be hanging around!

Dead Man's Hole intrigued me enough in my research to go looking for it, which was a bit of a task in and of itself. Allen and

I were following the only directions we could locate (which were vague), and realized that we had passed the site several times before finally finding our way. A path lined with large stones led us off the winding farm road, which was the only indication that we had found what we were looking for.

It is not immediately noticeable, but the actual site sits no more than a few dozen yards beyond the road. Loose gravel lines the path up to a historical marker, briefly describing the history of what lies just behind it. Dead Man's Hole was reportedly first discovered in 1821 by Ferdinand Lueders, an entomologist studying insects in the area. Several decades later, it would become known as a popular dumping ground for many unfortunate souls, including Unionists who were killed during the Civil War. It was widely rumored that the bodies of at least seventeen people were tossed into the cave, which stretches seven feet across and reaches a depth of over one hundred and fifty feet into the ground. Only three bodies recovered from the cave have ever been positively identified, while the rest of those presumed dead remain a mystery.

An oak tree that once towered over Dead Man's Hole was rumored to bear the marks left by ropes used for hangings. I doubt that neither the cave nor the tree was intended by Mother Nature to serve such gruesome purposes, but as history so often shows us, human beings are creatures of mass consumption who tend to use up any resources they can find—this cave being no exception.

In August 1872, a man known as Benjamin McKeever noticed a neighbor's dog out snapping at the heels of his horses, and became so annoyed by it that he thought he would take matters into his own hands and fire shots at the dog. The pet belonged to a nearby African-American man, and McKeever (a reportedly proud racist) took no issue with attempting to shoot the animal. The dog's owner was also shot at when he went to

Dead Man's Hole
(April Slaughter)

intercede, but was unharmed. He and his friends were angered over the incident and went after McKeever himself for revenge. Naturally, when his body came up missing, local law enforcement paid a visit to Dead Man's Hole and found some of his personal belongings hanging partially down into the cave. His body was recovered a short time later, and those accused of his murder were subsequently punished.

Settlers in the area knew the natural fissure to be a popular dumping ground, but as it accumulated a large amount of noxious gas, it was almost impossible to fully explore the underground cavern at the time. As technology progressed, the invention and use of gas masks made it possible for the Texas Speleological Society to map out the cave in 1968. Land owner Ona Lou Roper initially allowed qualified spelunkers down into the cave for exploration. Her husband's family had purchased the land in the 1920s, and they have been ranching on it ever since. Mrs. Roper eventually donated six acres of land that surrounds Dead Man's Hole to the county for preservation, and assisted in erecting the historical marker visitors see today.

The cave has since been sealed off to prevent harm to anyone curious enough to climb down into it, as well as to any animals that might be wandering nearby. The "hanging tree" has been removed as well, and much of the surrounding brush has been cleared. Scattered limestone rocks and a small patch of brush near the cave's entrance are all that remain.

As Allen and I walked the boulder-lined path up to Dead Man's Hole one sunny and humid afternoon, Allen asked me an interesting question.

"Do you hear anything?" he asked.

"What do you mean?" I replied.

"It's completely silent out here. It shouldn't be. I can't hear a bird . . . insects . . . anything making noise out here," he said.

I stood still and began to pay attention to my surroundings. He was right—I didn't hear a single thing. There was an eerie calm about the place, and it seemed a bit strange.

"I don't hear anything either," I said. "I'm sure we will. It's probably nothing more than a coincidence that we happened to notice."

We had turned on our digital recorder as we got out of our car, and decided to let it rest on top of the granite historical marker while we took a look around. I walked down a small slope that led to the entrance of the cave and sat on one of the boulders. Allen began to snap photographs and was no more than about five yards away when I heard the sound of a rock being thrown and landing close by. I looked to see where it was, or where it might have come from, but I saw nothing. For a moment, I thought Allen might have been playing around and decided to chuck a pebble at me, but he had his back turned to me and was too far away to have done it. A few minutes later, the exact same thing happened. I heard the same sound, but once again, I could not see the source.

I spent nearly twenty minutes sitting at the top of the cave, and for over half of that time, I got the impression that someone was trying to get my attention, or may have just been teasing me. Either way, I was never able to figure out what was going on.

Allen came back from taking pictures and sat down beside me on the boulder.

"What sorts of things have reportedly happened out here?" he asked.

I replied by telling him that several paranormal investigators had made trips to Dead Man's Hole to document any ongoing activity. Katrina Kindred and her partner Kelli Lindsay with Austin Paranormal had been warned by a psychic associate of theirs that Dead Man's Hole had a "serious energy pull" they needed to be careful of while conducting their investigation.

"When we got there, almost all of our equipment failed," said Katrina.

"We had two video recorders that had been charging over twenty-four hours, and a brand new pack of batteries," she continued. "One video recorder never even turned on, and the other went dead in about a minute. When we opened the battery package, all eight of the brand new batteries had been drained. The only thing that worked was our audio recorders."

In digging a little deeper, I also found that several other teams had been out to Dead Man's Hole in an attempt to document paranormal phenomena. Wendy Wilkins and Jennifer Trout of the Travis County Ghost Hunters have also spent nights out at the cave's entrance and have been able to capture disembodied voices each time. One voice seems to give an indecipherable response to a request to tug on a rope Wendy and Jennifer had lowered into the cave from a small opening at the top. Another of these recordings sounds as if it may be the voice of a small child humming softly somewhere nearby.

According to their website, the Travis County Ghost Hunters have repeatedly captured these same voices on their subsequent visits, leading them to believe that Dead Man's Hole is manifesting residual activity—a playback of sorts, an imprint of a moment in time that repeats itself and does not directly interact with the living.

When it came time for us to leave, we realized we had spent nearly two hours at Dead Man's Hole, and that the strange silence we noticed when we first arrived was still lingering. It was as if we had been sitting inside a bubble that nothing could infiltrate. It was very strange to me, as I have never before encountered that sort of quiet in the outdoors, especially in the middle of a warm and humid day in Texas.

Dead Man's Hole was once a good place to "get rid" of someone. It's bad enough to think about all of the poor souls who lost their lives and were then thrown into the abyss of the cave, but as we know so little about the exact circumstances surrounding these people, imagine for a moment if one (or more) of them had actually been tossed in there alive? No one knows for sure just how many bodies fell into the darkness, but I know one thing is certain—today, something is reaching out from it.

CHAPTER 17

Driskill Hotel
AUSTIN

Driskill Hotel exterior *(April Slaughter)*

JESSE LINCOLN DRISKILL purchased a city block in the heart of Austin in 1885 for $7,500 and set out to construct his dream—the Driskill Hotel. The construction cost $400,000, an exorbitant amount of money in those days. The hotel first opened its doors to guests on December 20, 1886. Mr. Driskill and his family had amassed a fortune in the cattle business, but subsequently lost it after three thousand of their herd perished in a freeze late in the spring of 1888. The hotel became too much of a financial burden that year, and Mr. Driskill was forced to sell it to Doc Day. Two years later, Driskill died of a stroke. A life-sized portrait of him was hung in the hotel lobby, where it remains today. He truly loved his hotel, and some say he died of a broken heart shortly after suffering its loss.

In 1895, Major George W. Littlefield purchased the hotel for $106,000 and vowed that it would never close again. He was a successful cattle baron, served as the president of the Texas Rangers, and also worked in banking. When he acquired the hotel, he made additions that included steam heating, electric lighting, and several upgrades to the guest rooms. He also opened a bank in the lobby of the hotel, and the original vault and door are still intact.

Psychic healers and medicine men began to make frequent appearances at the hotel in 1909, attracting a large number of people in search of a magical elixir or a glimpse into their futures. Several political figures also utilized the property for various events. Texas politician Lyndon B. Johnson and his future wife Lady Bird enjoyed their first date dining at the Driskill. In 1948, he awaited results of his U.S. senate race against Coke Stevenson in the Jim Hogg suite—a race that Johnson ultimately won.

Ownership of the hotel has changed several times over the last century, and it has continually undergone major renovations with nearly every new owner. Millions of dollars have been spent to keep this beautifully historic building up-to-date and one of the most prestigious hotels in Texas.

Allen took me on my first trip to Austin when I was asked to present at a Ghostology Radio event with my friends Brian and Anna Marie Byers late in 2008. Allen mentioned that the Driskill was nearby, and that it was rumored to be haunted by several different entities. His stepsister Suzi had worked at the hotel a number of years earlier and recounted several of her experiences to him. If I was going to Austin, I thought, I was staying at the Driskill. I researched what I could about ghostly encounters and requested a night in one of their haunted rooms.

The exterior of the hotel literally took my breath away when we arrived at the Driskill. It was pristine and ornate. From the moment I stepped inside, I was mesmerized by just how beautiful and elegant the hotel was. It was instantly fascinating; I wanted to explore every inch of it.

Mike Kemp, director of sales and marketing for the Driskill, met us in the lobby to discuss all of the paranormal happenings in different areas of the building.

"We hear ghost stories from guests quite often here," he said. "Some of them get really excited when they have taken pictures and an odd shadow or orb shows up in them."

Mr. Driskill himself is believed to haunt the hotel as he took great pride in it when he was alive. He has been seen many times relaxing in the lobby and lounge areas reading the paper, occasionally smoking a cigar and smiling at guests as they pass by.

The ghost of a four-year-old girl haunts the grand staircase leading from the mezzanine level to the lobby. She was the daughter of a U.S. senator visiting the hotel. As the story goes, the girl ran down the staircase after the ball she had been playing with slipped from her grasp. Both she and the ball went tumbling down the steps—an accident she did not survive. Staff and guests often hear her energetic laughter as well as the sound of an unseen ball bouncing down the staircase. During her years as an employee at the Driskill, my sister-in-law Suzi said she had seen the apparition of the little girl run through the lobby on more than one occasion.

Another popular story adding to the mystique of the hotel is that of the "Suicide Bride." Devastated by a broken engagement, she checked herself into a fourth-floor room at the Driskill for a quiet respite. After a brief and expensive shopping excursion courtesy of her ex-fiancé's credit cards, the unwed bride returned to the hotel carrying several packages to her room. Sadly, her shopping trip was not enough to help her forget her grief. She entered her guest room bath, lay down in the tub, and shot herself in the stomach, using a pillow to muffle the sound of the gunshot. A housekeeper discovered the body after becoming concerned when she noticed that the young woman hadn't left her room in several days.

Some believe that the Suicide Bride still haunts her room at the Driskill, making herself known to guests by knocking on the walls and moving objects to different locations. Could I get her to manifest if I stayed in that very room myself? Luckily, I had the chance to find out.

When Allen and I returned to the hotel after the event earlier that evening, we spent some time talking about how hurt this woman must have been, and how sorry we felt that she had endured such a heartbreak. We were both sitting on the bed when we heard a whimper near the closet. Allen immediately opened the closet doors and looked around but found no explanation. We heard the strange whimper twice more over a period of nearly two hours before we decided to turn in for the night.

At about 1:15 in the morning, something poking the bottom of my right foot suddenly awakened me. I quickly sat up in bed, but my eyes could not adjust well enough in the dark to see if anyone had been there. It was not a slight poke and I waited for the sensation to return, but it never did. I fell back to sleep without further incident that night.

The next morning, Allen and I went to have breakfast in the hotel's café. After our meal, we casually strolled around the lobby and admired all of the little architectural details throughout the lobby and the mezzanine level. As we stepped into the elevator to return to our room, we were both instantly covered in goose bumps. A sensation washed over us at the exact same moment that felt like something was crawling on our skin from our feet to the tops of our heads. We had no obvious explanation for the event. We stood there stunned and just looked at each other.

"Do you feel that?" I asked.

"I can't help but feel it," he said. "This is just too bizarre!"

The sensation and goose bumps quickly subsided as we approached the fourth floor, and we stepped off the elevator wondering what exactly it was that we had just experienced. It wasn't until weeks later that I learned the elevators in the hotel have long been the center of paranormal curiosity, as several people have reported strange occurrences in them.

As we gathered our things in preparation to check out, Allen and I talked about how truly impressed with the hotel we were. It is truly one of the most amazing places we have ever visited. Upon checkout, we thanked the staff for how wonderfully they took care of us and promised we'd be back to visit when we could.

When we arrived home, I recounted our experiences to friends who were eager to hear about our stay at the Driskill Hotel. Our good friend and associate John Melchior from California has often stayed at the hotel while traveling for business, and explained that he too had experiences there that he could

Driskill Hotel lobby
(April Slaughter)

not explain. On one particular evening, John had been watching television in his room on the fourth floor when he decided it was time to try to get some sleep.

"I turned off the TV and half an hour later it just came back on," he said. "An hour or so passed and once again the set turned itself on."

Another friend of mine, Ben Borth, relayed an experience to me that was unlike any other I had heard in regard to paranormal occurrences in the hotel. He had also occupied a room on the infamous fourth floor.

"The atmosphere, especially if you're staying in the historic section of the hotel, really has the potential to creep you out," he said. "There are pictures in the hallways of people who are now dead and mood music on the clock radios in the rooms."

Knowing he had experienced something even more frightening, I asked him to share the details with me.

"It wasn't so much an experience as it was a very intense dream," said Ben. "It was one of those dreams where you feel like you have actually woken up but are still in fact asleep. It began with me lying in bed when someone started pounding on the door.

"I jumped out of bed and through the door I could hear the maid yelling at me to get out of the room because I had slept through my check out time. She yelled, 'GET OUT!' to which I quickly replied, 'OK!' while I was scrambling to assemble all of my stuff. I opened the door and the maid was in the hallway with her hand around the neck of a friend of mine, pinning him up against the wall. Just as she turned to look at me, I woke up.

"When I got up the next morning, I looked at a dead person's picture there on the wall and I could have sworn it was the maid I had seen the night before in my dream."

Ben told me that in the few times he has returned to the Driskill, he has never been able to get a full night's sleep, and yet it remains one of his favorite places to visit.

My stay at the Driskill Hotel is one I will not soon forget, as it far exceeded any expectation I had before arriving. The staff and accommodations are phenomenal, as are the stories of those who still hold a connection to the hotel from the other side of the veil. Should you ever have the opportunity to visit, take some time to soak in the beauty of the hotel, enjoy a delicious meal in the café, and relax in your fourth floor guest room—that is, if you can. You never know who might come knocking on your door.

Spotlight on Ghosts:
The Capitol Haunting

There is the perception among paranormal enthusiasts that ghosts make themselves known only in the dark, late-night hours. Nothing could be further from the truth. In fact, there are places where specters are seen and experienced in the middle of the day as well as at night, like the Capitol building in Austin.

Visitors to the grounds have unexpectedly encountered the ghost of Governor Edmund Jackson Davis (1827–1883) staring out of the building from a flrst- oor window, most often with a cold stare and blank expression that sends a chill up the spine. He not only haunts the interior of the building, he is also repeatedly seen walking about the grounds. Those who cross his path are caught in his unbroken stare until they pass, and then he vanishes from sight.

Another resident of the Capitol building is rumored to be the spirit of State Comptroller Robert M. Love, who was gunned down by a disgruntled former employee as he sat working at his desk in 1903. He walks the halls, often disappearing into walls and reappearing in different sections of the building. He too has stopped to meet the gaze of visitors and employees, scaring them as they try to go about their business.

Misty days on the Capitol grounds seem particularly active, as several unidentifled apparitions have been witnessed walking the path up to the building. Why on a foggy, dreary day? No one quite knows for sure, but the atmosphere this type of weather creates is certainly enough not only to attract the souls of the dead, but also those eager to see and interact with them.

Whether the sky is fllled with sun or covered in a canopy of clouds on the day of your visit, it is certainly worth it to make the trip to Austin. The Capitol building is a beautiful piece of architecture to behold; a place where the history of Texas has been honored and shared by not only the living, but by those who have long since passed on.

CHAPTER 18

Caldwell County Jail Museum
LOCKHART

Caldwell County Jail Museum exterior
(April Slaughter)

IN NEARLY EVERY COMMUNITY, there is a place tucked away among the homes, churches, and businesses that the locals whisper about; a building with history, whether good or bad, where people have seen and heard things that defy explanation. Scary stories are fascinating to all of us, but seeking them out to experience them firsthand can be a little frightening. There are those who keep their distance out of fear, while some of us are driven to conquer our fears. We seek out the places with creepy reputations. In doing so, I discovered this historic jail.

My friends Brian and Anna Marie Byers live in Lockhart, where they broadcast their popular radio show *Ghostology* every Saturday night on CBS Radio. Their investigative group, the Emania Research Facility, is an affiliate of The Paranormal Source, Inc. and had already been to the Caldwell County Jail on several occasions to see if they could validate any of the paranormal phenomena that reportedly occurs there. Whenever we discussed locations in Texas that intrigued them the most, Brian and Anna Marie would speak about the jail. My curiosity about the place grew, and when I was invited to speak at a *Ghostology*-sponsored event in Lockhart, I saw a golden opportunity to see the building they had told me so much about.

The jail is an impressive red brick, castle-like structure just off the town's main road. This, however, was not the first jail for Caldwell County; it was the fourth. The original jail was a log cabin building constructed in 1855. After only three years in operation, the jail burnt to the ground and took with it many of the historical county records that were stored inside. In 1908, a man named T.S. Hodges constructed the building you see today.

The Caldwell County Jail Museum now inhabits the building, which closed as an active holding facility in the early 1970s when a newer and more modern structure was erected. The old jail was recorded as a Texas Historic Landmark in 1977, and has been impressively preserved and opened to the community.

The jail has four floors. The basement, which is primarily used for storage, is not accessible to the public. The main floor, which originally served as the living quarters for the local sheriff and his family, is now the reception area, where visitors are greeted before taking a tour. Various household items that were common in the past are displayed here. The third and fourth floors contain a total of fifteen cells made of concrete and steel. One cell at the top of the building sits alone, and was used for solitary confinement.

On our initial trip into Lockhart, I immediately took notice of the jail and asked Allen to stop the car so that I could take a few pictures before heading to the event with our friends. The museum was not open and I did not have the opportunity to look inside just then, so we made arrangements with Brian and Anna Marie to come back another time for an official investigation of the building.

When my husband and I finally made it back out to Lockhart a few months later, we sat down with Brian and Anna Marie to talk about their experiences at the jail, and I had never heard a story quite likes theirs before.

"We conducted a nighttime investigation with our team from Emania," said Brian. "We really did not know what to expect out of the evening, but it turned out to be a pretty productive investigation for us.

"We had set up our audio to record on the third floor, and while none of us heard it at the time, we later discovered what sounded like a baby cooing in the background."

"Were there any children with you on the night of your investigation?" I asked.

"No, only adults were there," answered Brian.

I silently wondered why a baby would have been heard on tape, and then thought it may have something to do with the families that had once lived in the building to take care of the jail and its prisoners—but there was more to the story.

"This is where it gets strange," Brian continued. "Anna Marie was about twelve weeks pregnant with our son Ashlind at the time. We listened to that baby vocalization on the recording dozens of times before Ashlind was born, and we really didn't know what to make of it."

The Byers' baby boy was now about eight months old, and when I listened to his voice and compared it to the recording, they sounded identical. Granted, a lot of babies would probably sound very similar on a recording, but in listening to it myself I could not make any distinction between Ashlind and the disembodied voice.

There is no record of a small child dying in the jail, so finding a more plausible explanation for the recording is difficult. I couldn't find an answer, but it certainly sparked several more questions. Could it be Ashlind's voice on the recording? If it is, how is that possible? He hadn't even been born yet. And what did he have to do with the jail? It just goes to show you that when you create a theory on how the paranormal might work, you really have no clue and you have to begin looking at things from completely different angles.

As fascinating as this occurrence was, it was not the only thing the Byers and their team encountered that night. Anna Marie had been sitting on the third floor when she saw a shadowy figure move about the cells.

"Are you the sheriff that used to live in this jail?" she asked, hoping to elicit some sort of response from the apparition.

She received one. Immediately following her question, an EVP was captured of a woman's voice saying, "No . . . please help. Someone is burning!"

A recorder left alone in the fourth floor solitary confinement cell had also recorded an EVP of a very deep voice saying, "It's burning."

Who were these people, and were they talking about the fire that destroyed the original jailhouse building in 1858? No one knows.

My long-awaited trip inside finally came, and both Brian and Anna Marie were there to see if any of the phenomena they had experienced would repeat itself, or if we would encounter something new altogether.

Allen and Brian thought it might be a good idea to use "ghost box" devices that had not been previously attempted in the jail. Brian and Anna Marie brought what is known as the Shack Hack—a small, portable modified radio from Radio Shack that can be used much in the same way as the Frank's Box or Mini-Box devices. After running the Shack Hack for several minutes on the third floor and not hearing anything significant come through, Allen suggested we use Frank's Box #37 in solitary confinement upstairs.

We all took turns asking questions, hoping someone would give us a clear answer. Nothing came through at first, until I turned questions into statements.

"If any of you from the past are still here, we'd really appreciate hearing from you," I said.

Much to my amazement, a clear and consistent male voice was heard over the constantly moving radio band.

"We don't like it here, April," he said.

"When will you be released from the jail?" asked Brian.

"Oh, we're not," the radio responded.

Nothing else came through, though we kept asking a barrage of different questions. Whoever had been speaking to us through the Frank's Box wasn't talking anymore. After a few more minutes with no response, we thought we would try again on the floor just beneath us. Allen set the box up on one of the empty cell bunks and hung the antenna wire close to the nearest window to ensure a clear radio signal.

Several minutes passed, and we were not hearing anything we believed was relevant. As a group, we began talking amongst ourselves while the box kept running in the background. We were anxious to hear anything more that might come through.

Caldwell County Jail Museum holding cells (April Slaughter)

"Is it hard talking through this radio, guys?" asked Brian.

"Can't control it," responded the box.

"Is it the box you have a hard time controlling?" asked Brian, hoping to clarify the response.

"Yes!" said a voice emphatically, and then the box fell silent.

Two distinctly different investigative experiences occurred in the Caldwell County Jail, both equally active and impressive. When I try to describe events such as these to people, they often ask me, "Why don't the spirits just tell you their name and story outright? Why are there usually only bits and pieces that come through?"

My theory is this: While the living may occasionally occupy the same space as the dead, our process of communication may work well for us, but not for those on the other side of the veil. Their reality may be entirely different than ours, and I am not convinced that it is any easier for them to overcome obstacles than it is for us. Finding a way to use our environments and the avenues for communication available to us isn't always easy.

We can set up as much technical equipment as we like, and document everything we can perceive to the very last detail. Does that mean we have covered all of our bases? No. For every genuine paranormal experience I have, I often wonder how many are happening around me that I am not yet able to detect.

When we concluded our investigation, we all left with the impression that we definitely had not been alone while wandering around the jail. Someone, quite possibly several "someones," had tried to reach out and communicate with us. Overall, it was a pretty amazing experience.

Allen and I thanked Brian and Anna Marie for their time and assistance with our visit, packed up, and headed for home.

As I learn and progress in my search for the unexplained, I will continue to visit those places that have consistently proven to me that there is life beyond death, and the Caldwell County Jail

Museum is right there on my list of places to continue the work. Whether it is haunted by the tormented souls of those who once served their sentences there, or by the families who did their duty in taking care of them and the community, I'll be back to talk with them again and to witness their stories unfold.

CHAPTER 19

Von Minden Hotel

SCHULENBURG

**Von Minden Hotel exterior
(April Slaughter)**

"WHERE ON EARTH
IS SCHULENBURG?"
asked Allen.

"You're a native Texan
and you're asking *me*?" I
replied.

Thank heaven for
technology and our ability
to plug any city or address
into a GPS system to help
us find our way around.
Where would we be with-
out it? Lost. Schulenburg,
Texas, isn't a huge thriv-
ing metropolis like Dal-
las, Austin, or Houston,
so Allen and I needed all
of the help we could get in
locating it.

The Von Minden Hotel
had long been on my list of "must see" places, and finally making my way out to it was an adventure all its own. Its haunted
reputation and lack of modern amenities was a huge draw for me.
Here I was depending on modern technology to get me to a place
where time had virtually stood still for so many years. Go figure.

The building was constructed in 1927 and first opened its
doors as a theatre. The hotel portion would open just a year later

with forty guest rooms. Today, it remains the only surviving hotel in Texas that houses an operating theatre.

When we pulled up in front of the hotel, Allen pointed out the old neon sign reading "HOTEL" with only the "O" and "T" lights still functioning. A slight flicker made me wonder if those last two letters would soon be on their way out as well. The entrance door was wide open, so we walked into the lobby where several people sat watching television. I glanced over to the check-in counter and noticed that no one was there. *Maybe they were helping a guest,* I thought. *Surely they'll be back soon.*

We introduced ourselves to the guests in the lobby, and learned that they were regulars who stayed at the Von Minden every year during their participation in the Multiple Sclerosis MS-150 fundraising bike ride from Houston to Austin. Deborah Kurc had been coming here for the past six years, and found the hotel eerily charming.

"By the time we arrive here at the hotel, we're normally exhausted from the ride, but today was the first time in twenty-five years that the ride was cancelled due to the rain, so we're just waiting it out," said Deborah.

"In all of the years you've stayed here, have you ever experienced anything strange?" I asked.

"Yes, actually. Sometimes I'll wake up in the middle of the night around three o'clock in the morning because it sounds like someone is dragging heavy furniture around," she said. "By that time, everyone is asleep and there would be no reasonable explanation for sounds like that. I never have figured out what's going on with that."

Deborah asked if we would like to see her room, and escorted us up the stairs to the next floor of the hotel. As we walked down the hallway, I noticed that several of the rooms were closed up or stacked with storage. Old sections of wallpaper were slowly peeling away from the walls, there were cobwebs aplenty, and if you wanted to capture a picture full of orbs, this would be the place to do it as every step we took produced a small cloud of dust around our feet.

There was nothing fancy about Deborah's room, but I could definitely see what attracted her to this hotel year after year— it was an adventure! Every nook and cranny of this place had unique character and fun little things scattered around to discover. Allen was eager to see the upper floors as well, so Deborah took us on a short unofficial tour.

A locked door stood at one end of the hallway, and just above it a sign read "HARD TIMES." Apparently, this had been a restaurant and bar in the not-so-distant past. I wondered where it got its name, but decided that I probably already knew. I was sure it was a place that people went to have a drink and perhaps numb their sorrows, at least for a little while.

"I wonder where Bill is," said Deborah.

"Is Bill the owner?"

"Yes, Bill Pettit is his name. He's one of the nicest people you'd ever meet. I am sure he is wandering around downstairs somewhere."

As we descended the staircase, I wondered if Bill would be back at the lobby desk. No such luck. Twenty minutes or so passed as we spoke with the group still watching television, and an older gentleman outside walked just in front of the open entrance door.

"That's Bill!" said Deborah.

I grabbed Allen's hand and we quickly walked outside.

"Hi, are you Bill Pettit, the owner?" I asked.

"Why, yes I am, young lady," he said.

First, I was grateful for the "young" comment, as I had just turned thirty years old the day before, and I was not at all happy about it. Second, I had finally pinned down the owner and I was excited to talk to him and learn more about the Von Minden.

After brief introductions and a bit of explanation for our visit, I overwhelmed Bill with a great deal many questions.

"How long have you owned the hotel?" I asked.

"Since 1979," he replied.

I asked if he lived in the building, which he indicated that he did not. Several members of his family did, however, in three separate apartments inside. He did have an office on one of the upper floors, but he no longer used it.

Bill told Allen and me that he was a retired criminal defense attorney who had often defended those on trial for murder. I mentioned that I would imagine that to be difficult, but Bill saw it as just a job and nothing more. He couldn't afford to become emotionally involved or it would have consumed him. The hotel in which he had spent so many years since his retirement was haunted; could some of the resident spirits be tied to his past as their lawyer or the victims of those on trial? I didn't see why not. Spirits are not bound by the physical world. Maybe some of the paranormal activity here could be attributed to those involved in his courtroom past.

"We've got ghosts," he continued, "but I only know for sure who one of them is."

"Who?"

"My late wife. She'd battled cancer, and died in February of 2002," he said. "If I carry a drink around with me inside, she knocks it out of my hand. I know it's her because she and I were married just days shy of fifty years, and she didn't like me walking around with drinks."

I could tell he missed her a great deal, but found it endearing that he spoke with humor about the mysterious little mishaps he believed her to be responsible for.

Several online sources also describe a tragic event that is said to have occurred in room #37. As the story goes, an injured World War II paratrooper came to the hotel on his way home to his family after having been declared "missing in action." When he arrived at the hotel, he was given several letters written by the woman he loved, and he began reading them out of sequence. Upon reading a letter in which the woman wrote that she was leaving him, the distraught veteran jumped to his death. Had he read the other letters that followed, he'd have discovered her regret and learned that she still loved him and wanted to be with him. Were these lovers forever tied to the Von Minden? Who really knew for certain?

As our conversation with Bill continued, we became even more curious about the activity others encountered in the hotel.

"What have some of your guests experienced here?" asked Allen.

"After my wife passed away, I was in the Hard Times with one of the guests, who was taking photographs. When the pictures were developed, you could clearly see the figure of a woman in one of them. It looked just like my wife standing there," he said.

He also went on to describe an incident where two young boys had come to the hotel with their father, and while his attention was drawn elsewhere, the boys climbed out onto the fire escape from one of the upper-level windows. Bill had asked them to come back in due to safety concerns, and as the boys climbed back inside, their father snapped a photograph of them in the hallway.

"The picture clearly showed a man standing next to the boys that wasn't visible when the photo was taken," said Bill.

"I would love to see these pictures!" I exclaimed.

"Let me tell you about the pictures," he said. "People take them and bring them into us. I put them in different places, and they come up missing. People are so intrigued by them that they take them."

Von Minden Hotel interior. Note "666" on the register.
(April Slaughter)

What a shame that is! I asked Bill if he was open to the idea of others coming to the hotel to investigate the reported paranormal phenomena.

"I've had several groups out, and it's always interesting to see what they come up with," he said. "Some people come and tell me they don't believe the hotel is haunted. That's okay, I'm not out to convince anybody. If you believe there are ghosts here, they're here. If you don't, then they're not. Anyone interested is invited to visit and come to their own conclusions."

Whether you stop in to stay the night, to see a movie, or just to walk the historic hallways of the Von Minden Hotel, be sure to say hello to Bill when you go—that is, if you can find him. You just might run in to someone else you didn't expect.

Spotlight on Ghosts:
Goliad

The ghosts of Goliad are as much a presence today as they were in 1836, when General Antonio Lopez de Santa Anna ordered the execution of revolutionaries who had lost the Battle of Caleto—one of the most significant of all Texas battles with Mexican troops. Colonel James W. Fannin, Jr. held his men at Presidio La Bahia at Goliad, knowing that the Alamo had already fallen, in defiance that would ultimately cost him and his men their lives. Fannin was in a difficult position as he had worked tirelessly to fortify Goliad. He and his men were eager to face and fight the Mexican army, led by José de Urrea, which was quickly advancing toward them.

Fannin had approximately three hundred men to defend their position, while Urrea's forces grew to nearly one thousand. After a short period of fighting, Fannin realized that defeating the Mexican army was nearly impossible and, for the sake of the wounded, sought terms of an honorable surrender. He asked that his men be allowed to surrender and be taken as prisoners of war, which meant that they would be treated for their wounds and eventually paroled to the United States. Urrea could not agree to such terms, yet Fannin led his men to believe they would be cared for and eventually sent home.

Texas doctors were forced to leave their own men dying on the battlefield, many of whom were left suffering for days, and tend to the Mexican wounded. Urrea advanced toward Guadalupe Victoria to secure it as well, and he wrote to Santa Anna on behalf of the Texas wounded at Goliad asking for clemency. The request was denied and Colonel José Nicolás de la Portilla was commanded to execute Fannin's entire command on Palm Sunday, March 27, 1836. This would become known as the Goliad Massacre; 342 men lost their lives.

It has been said that a distinctly negative spirit resides within the walls of Presidio La Bahia today, and that in order to escape its wrath one must remain extremely still to avoid attention until the apparition (said to resemble a robed and hooded monk) passes by. It is also rumored that shadowy figures march with their guns along the mission grounds, and the barely audible sounds of disembodied conversations can be heard throughout the mission. The apparition of a grief-stricken woman has also been seen wandering through the cemetery, seemingly in search of a long-lost love or family member.

Paranormal sightings in Goliad are an active reminder of all that was lost in Texas' past. Take the time to visit the old town, and you may come face-to-face with a ghostly piece of history.

East Texas

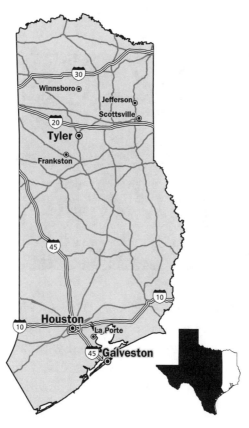

Frankston
Dabbs Cemetery

Houston
Spaghetti Warehouse

Jefferson
Ghost Train of Jefferson
The Grove

La Porte
USS *Texas*

Scottsville
Scottsville Cemetery

Tyler
Crystals Rock Shop

Winnsboro
Oklea Mansion Bed & Breakfast

CHAPTER 20

Oaklea Mansion Bed & Breakfast
WINNSBORO

Oaklea Mansion exterior from the gardens (April Slaughter)

I OFTEN WONDER HOW DIFFERENT life must have been during the early 1900s, as the turn of the century ushered in a new and exciting era filled with ambition, elegance, and beauty in America. As time progresses, this history is often forgotten as we focus our energies on moving forward with our own accomplishments. The old adage, "out with the old, in with the new" seems all too true today. I have always felt that in order to truly appreciate the present, one must take a step back and remember the past.

Whenever I happen upon a place that remains almost as it was during the younger years of this country, I try to imagine who might have been there before me and the types of joys and struggles they encountered during their lifetime. Oaklea Mansion was a pleasing discovery. When I set out to learn its story, I knew something special was in store for me.

The colonial-style home was originally built in 1903 by Mr. Marcus Dewitt Carlock, Sr. He was a successful attorney who had been involved in many political ventures, and often entertained the politically elite of the time. The Carlock home was recorded as a Texas Historical Landmark in 1966; a marker bearing a brief history of the house is proudly displayed beside the front door.

Current owner Norma Wilkinson was born and raised in Winnsboro, and knew the Carlock family prior to purchasing the home in 1996. At the time, Mrs. Carlock—lovingly known as Rhea—was 89 years old and bedridden, unable to leave her home due to osteoporosis. She had come to Winnsboro a young bride and spent the rest of her life in this house, which she so dearly loved. Her husband had died just the year before, and Mrs. Carlock asked Norma to buy the home so that it would be well taken care of after her passing. Norma purchased the mansion and worked tirelessly to add those changes and additions Mrs. Carlock had always wanted for the home, but had never been able to accomplish because her husband preferred it to remain as plain as possible.

During the last three months of Mrs. Carlock's life, Norma was there every day to visit her and to work on the house. While she did not survive long enough to see the mansion fully completed, Norma is sure that Mrs. Carlock is pleased with the way it turned out. Norma and her husband live in the home, but have also opened it to guests as the Oaklea Mansion Bed & Breakfast.

Many visitors to the mansion and its grounds have reported strange experiences during their stay, and paranormal teams have also investigated the home, finding that legitimate activity was indeed occurring there. Allen and I made arrangements to spend a night, and to discuss these experiences with Norma.

"Do you believe your home is haunted?" I asked.

"Well, I am a bit of a skeptic," said Norma. "But I do believe in the possibility that it might be. I had one guest that spent a night in a room I call the 'Angel Suite.' When she came down for breakfast the next morning, she asked me if we had a cat in the house. I told her that, no, we did not . . . and I was curious why she asked. She told me that during the night, she felt what she thought might have been a cat jumping up onto the bed and rubbing up against her back. She has stayed with us a few times since then, but refuses to be placed in that room now."

A year later, another guest of the B&B stayed in the Angel Suite and reported that she too felt the presence of a cat on the bed. Neither of the two women had known each other, and Norma had not discussed the previous incident with anyone.

Just prior to Mrs. Carlock's passing, the woman who had been living with her to oversee her care woke up one night to check on her, when something odd caught her attention.

"Rhea had been restless, so Ms. Hammond [the caretaker] went to look in on her. She told me that she felt they had had a visitor in the night," said Norma.

"When Ms. Hammond approached the back bathroom here on the first floor," Norma continued, "she could smell the distinct scent of sweet tobacco smoke in the air. Mrs. Carlock attributed it to her late husband (who used to smoke tobacco), saying she believed 'Papa' was simply stopping by to check in on them."

The smell of tobacco smoke was also experienced by Norma's bookkeeper while Norma and her husband were away on vacation. The woman had been working at the computer when she thought she smelled smoke, which alarmed her and prompted her to thoroughly check the house for any problem. When she was unable to discover any potential danger, she returned to the computer to work and the smell of the tobacco smoke returned—

this time strong enough to scare her into immediately leaving the house.

Nearly nine years ago, Norma decided to construct a guest house on the grounds to accommodate more guests to the B&B. One evening, as a few individuals sat out on the balcony of the guest house, they looked over across the gardens below to see the misty apparition of a man walking on the lawn. They saw him for a few moments before he disappeared into thin air.

"Who do you think he might have been?" I asked Norma.

Entrance to Oaklea Mansion
(April Slaughter)

"If there are spirits here, I am sure one of them would have to be Mr. Carlock. I think he may be a little uneasy with all of the changes we have made to his home. I don't think he is unhappy, per se—maybe just a bit unsettled by the differences. I know Mrs. Carlock is probably very pleased," she said.

After having spoken with Allen and me about the history of the grounds, Norma escorted us to our room in the guest house for the night. She had given us the "English Rose" room, which was richly decorated in floral décor and had access to the balcony. As we were getting settled, I checked my cell phone for messages, and gently tossed it onto the bed next to Allen's. He and I have the same model of phone and there is nothing to outwardly identify which is which.

I was eager to look out over the beautifully landscaped gardens and ponds from the balcony while Allen had excused himself to the restroom.

A few minutes later, we were both out on the balcony admiring how peaceful the evening was when our conversation was interrupted by the sound of a door opening just to our left. We instinctively turned our heads to see who might be joining us, but no one was there. We waited a moment or two and went to see where the sound had come from, but no door to the balcony had been opened.

When we re-entered our room, I walked over to the bed to retrieve my phone and it was not there. Somehow, in the short time that had passed since we stepped outside, my phone had been placed back in its case and placed on the nightstand next to the bed. Allen told me he had noticed both of the phones on the bed before stepping out onto the balcony with me. How strange is it that whoever had picked up and placed my phone in its case on the nightstand knew which one was mine? Our guest room had been locked the entire time, so no one could have entered while we were outside.

As we prepared to turn in for the night, Allen and I talked about how lovely it was to be guests of Oaklea Mansion, and how pleased we would be to make a repeat visit sometime soon. After a few hours' sleep, Allen was jolted awake by the feeling of a hand gripping his left ankle. He sat up in bed and saw no one there, but maintains that someone or something had touched him. He waited for awhile, but sleep ultimately found him again and the remainder of the night was uneventfully peaceful.

Norma treated us to an elegant breakfast the next morning while we discussed our experiences from the night before. She listened and smiled intently as we spoke, and invited us to come back and visit anytime we were traveling in the east Texas area.

Over the years, having witnessed all types of strange phenomena, I have lost my fear or nervousness when events such
as those we experienced at Oaklea Mansion occur. I welcome
the interaction and the chances I have been given to determine
that just because something is invisible, it doesn't mean it isn't
there. For example, I cannot see the wind, yet I know when it
is blowing and can immediately identify the feeling. The paranormal often affects me in much the same way. Sometimes you
just know when you are in the presence of something spiritual,
and I believe wholeheartedly that Allen and I were not the only
guests of the Oaklea Mansion that day.

The amount of love and respect Norma has poured into this
home is evident from the first moment you arrive. If I were a
member of the Carlock family, I know I would enjoy being in
the home from either side of the veil.

CHAPTER 21

Crystals Rock Shop
TYLER

Crystals Rock Shop exterior (April Slaughter)

WHAT I LOVE MOST ABOUT THE PARANORMAL is that it's unpredictable. Anything can happen. Those of us who study the paranormal conjure up a myriad of theories based on what we research and experience, in hopes of gaining a little more understanding about how one factor might affect another. Some investigators believe that the only way to conduct an investigation is through purely scientific means, while others believe spirituality is more important.

Personally, I am stuck right in between the two ends of the spectrum. In my opinion, scientific data collection plays an important role in documenting legitimate paranormal phenomena. By the same token, however, I don't think that we as human beings are even close to creating a sure-fire way to prove one way or another with equipment alone that the "other side" truly exists. We all rely on our intuition in ordinary, everyday situations, and I try to pay attention to mine in those that might be paranormal as well. Just as I am often excited to try out a new piece of scientific equipment, I am always looking for new spiritual "tools" as well.

For years, I have read articles and books on the energetic healing and protective properties of rocks and crystals. The first specimen I went in search of was hematite—a stone that is believed to repel negativity. I purchased it in the form of an inexpensive band that I wore on my finger, and began taking it with me everywhere I went. Did it protect me from negativity? I'm not exactly sure, but I enjoyed wearing the ring and thought any talisman that represented a positive attitude and protection was worth bringing along.

I hadn't purchased any hematite in quite some time when I began discussing different rocks and their properties with Allen. I mentioned that I would like to find a place to purchase another piece, and one of our investigators, Buffy Clary, said she lived near a quaint little rock shop in Tyler that was sure to have anything I was looking for in regard to different stones and talismans. Crystals Rock Shop sits in a quiet residential neighborhood, and if it weren't for the small, nondescript sign out front, you wouldn't even know it was there.

Allen, Jerry Bowers, and I made a trip out to the shop one day to see what fun little trinkets we would find. We pulled up and parked in the gravel driveway that leads to a small converted garage adjacent to the house on the property. The entrance is a chain link fence, and just beyond the gate are several outdoor tables filled with large stones of every shape and color one could imagine. Next to the door stands a beautiful, tall wood carving of a wizard that looks as though he were keeping a wary eye on the inventory outside.

After we had looked around for a few brief moments, the lady at the counter welcomed us to the shop.

"Hello. Is there anything I can help you find?" she said.

"Yes, actually," I said. "I am looking for hematite. Would you happen to carry it?"

She assured me that she did, and proceeded to show me where it was located.

"Are you looking to use it for anything specific?" she asked.

"Yes, we'd like to have a piece or two to carry with us on paranormal investigations and such. Plus, I really love the way it looks and just like having it around."

"I'm Debi Lacey," she said. "It's nice to meet you."

Right in front of her on the counter sat a Teacup Chihuahua, obviously at home in his little dog bed and blanket.

"This is T.J. He's old and a bit ornery, but he helps me keep watch over the place."

As we all introduced ourselves, Debi seemed intrigued by the fact that we were investigators. What we thought would be a brief, ten- to fifteen-minute shopping trip turned into an almost hour-long visit. We looked at all sorts of stones, and read about their properties in several books available to peruse.

"You know, we have ghosts," said Debi. "I suspect I even know who they are."

Naturally intrigued, I listened as she began to tell us the history of the rock shop. Bill and Gean Wheless originally lived on the property and had run the shop for many years. Debi had come to work for the couple five years previously, and also helped to take care of Gean as she was getting older and could not adequately care for herself and the shop.

Gean was the first to pass on, and her husband Bill died a few years later. Debi has remained living in the house and keeps the shop open to the public every Friday and Saturday.

"One afternoon, a young lady came in and it was her very first visit here," said Debi. "She told me that she was able to see and communicate with the spirit of an older woman standing close by, and that the woman wanted me to pay more attention to the paperwork.

"Gean was very meticulous about her record keeping. I didn't pay much attention to the comment until it came back to bite me around tax time and I hadn't done as Gean had insisted. I keep on top of it now."

While Debi and I were chatting, Jerry and Allen had both found a few items they wanted to purchase and approached the glass case that Debi was standing behind. As Allen handed Debi a $20 bill, another customer in the store asked for her assistance. She went to place the money on the counter and it slipped from her hand and fell to the floor. Allen and Jerry had watched it fall, but a few moments later when Debi returned, the money was lying right in the middle of the counter.

"Things like this happen all of the time!" she exclaimed. "One of the biggest mysteries is what happens to my earrings as I am standing behind the counter. I'll come in wearing a pair, and then somehow my right earring will come up missing entirely. It's always the right one, and what's strange is I never find them again."

Debi told me that at one point, an individual in the store actually watched as the earring was lifted from her ear and dropped on the floor.

Interestingly enough, unusual activity is not restricted to the shop. The house on the property, while not open to the public, also has its share of spooky experiences. Bill and Gean's son Robert had lived in the home until recently, and he has a hard time making sense of an incident that occurred on his birthday just a couple of years back.

"It was my birthday, and I opened up the top drawer of my dresser to look for something when I found a card addressed to me inside," Robert said. "Funny thing is, I had been shuffling through that same drawer several times that day and the card had not been there. I opened it up and it was a birthday card signed by my mother."

Robert looked genuinely confused as he told us this story, and as our conversation progressed, we learned that these sorts of things got under his skin and he didn't much like discussing "the boogers," as he called them.

Debi never seems at all fazed by the activity, save for when it causes her a little frustration.

"When I close up the shop, I will come into the house and hang the keys on a hook so that I know exactly where they are when it's time to open up again," she said. "Oftentimes, I will go to get the keys and they will not be where I left them. I'll state out loud that I can't open the shop without those keys, and as I continue on with doing something else, they'll reappear right on that hook as if they had never been moved."

Debi also went on to tell us that a black mist has often been seen moving down the hallway of the house, and frightening her roommate Beth.

"Nearly every day, I will see shadow figures standing in my front room window from the outside of the house," she said. "It can be a bit unsettling, but I am never frightened by it."

During our first visit to Crystals Rock Shop, I noticed a table where three large white bowls were sitting. I asked what they were used for, and Debi explained to me that they were crystal singing bowls, used to clear the energy of whatever you placed inside of them. When a rubber mallet is gently moved around their rims, each exudes a different gentle tone.

I had come to the shop looking for something to help keep Allen and me clear of negativity during investigations, so I didn't think it could hurt to "bless" the hematite in one of them before we left. I had never seen or heard of anything like that before, and thought that even if it did nothing, it was still a neat thing to try.

"Those bowls have started singing on their own too," said Debi. "It has happened about four times now that I can recall, and it's always when I am the only one here to hear it and the mallet is sitting on the counter nowhere near them."

I half-jokingly asked if T.J., the elderly little dog, ever seemed to react to anything strange.

"Actually, yes," she said. "He used to do this very specific little dance just for Gean when she was alive that he'll occasionally do when there is no one else but me around. I'll catch him looking off somewhere doing that funny dance. He never does it for me; he only did it for her."

Crystals Rock Shop is another one of those little unexpected finds—a place you'd never think of when you hear stories of paranormal happenings. While it cannot be proven that the collection of rocks and gemstones in the shop attract paranormal activity, it certainly seems plausible given the spiritual power that many of the specimens are thought to possess.

Debi loves and maintains the rock shop, but she is convinced that she is not the only one making sure the business runs as it should. She believes that the spirit of her dear friend Gean is still an important presence in her life and in the lives of all of those who visit the quaint little shop.

Spotlight on Ghosts: The Bragg Light of the Ghost Road

Near Saratoga there is a long dirt road bordered with a canopy of trees. Originally known as Bragg Road, it has attracted a lot of attention over the years and is now called the Ghost Road of Hardin County. It is home to the Bragg Light—a nocturnal phenomenon that suggests something paranormal is occurring on the approximately eight-mile stretch of road.

The Sante Fe Railroad established a line in the Big Thicket in 1902 to transport people, animals, and goods to Beaumont. In 1934, many of the area's natural resources ran out and road crews were assigned to tear up the tracks and create a county road in their place. Over the course of the next few decades, stories began to circulate that the road was haunted; by whom or what is still unknown.

A strange misty light has been seen forming out of complete darkness and moving fluidly across the road for several minutes at a time. In recent years, several photos depict the Bragg Light, although many people argue about its source. Some speculate that it is the soul of a man who once lost his new bride to a mysterious murderer while staying at a hotel near the end of the Ghost Road endlessly searching for his long-lost love.

A more grisly explanation for the light is the story of a man who reportedly died a terrifying death by decapitation in a train wreck when the railroad was still in operation. It is said that his head was never found, and there are those who believe he will forever haunt the road looking for it.

On July 28, 1997, the County Commissioners Court designated the area as The Ghost Road Scenic Drive County Park in an effort to preserve it for future visitors and travelers.

Whatever is responsible for the Bragg Light is still unknown, but that doesn't keep the curious away. Muster up enough courage for a nighttime stroll down the old Ghost Road, and you just might solve the mystery for yourself.

CHAPTER 22

Dabbs Cemetery
FRANKSTON

**African-American side of Dabbs Cemetery
(April Slaughter)**

WHEN I WAS YOUNGER, my parents often thought it was strange of me to request a visit to the local cemeteries rather than playgrounds or parks. I have always been fascinated with them and find walking among the headstones to be a relaxing and tranquil experience.

My favorite cemeteries are those that seem to have been forgotten or neglected, as they have a mysterious character about them. I am drawn in by their uniqueness and the colorful histories they possess, oftentimes unknown by most people. I make a point to read the names of those that are legible on each headstone, and I feel a bit of sadness for those that are not. If a name is covered in debris, I will stop to brush it away. It is something I have always done, and my own special way of paying my respects.

As far back as I can remember, I have heard countless stories of haunted cemeteries wherever I have traveled, and Texas is no exception. In my experience, however, I think people tend to label cemeteries as haunted simply because of their obvious association with death; a subject that creates fear in many. People like to be scared, even if only briefly, and cemeteries often provide the perfect setting for such an experience.

Allen and I recently made a trip out to east Texas to visit several locations, including Dabbs Cemetery, a place I had learned about via the Internet. According to an article written by Bob Bowman, east Texas historian and author, a man once mistaken for dead was buried alive in the cemetery, only to dig his way out a short time later. It is said that he made his way to a nearby home, where he then died. In an effort to ensure that he would not be able to escape his grave a second time, the locals constructed a cage of wooden stakes directly above his burial site. No evidence of who this man was or where the grave might be exists today, but locals still tell the story and believe that he may be one of many restless spirits seen roaming about the grounds at night.

Several people I spoke to about the cemetery believe that being on the grounds after dusk can have dire consequences and consider any amount of time spent there as a rite of passage. A young local woman told me that she and a group of high school seniors had taken a trip to the vicinity shortly after graduation. As they approached the cemetery that evening, the students saw the apparition of a woman in a white dress floating above the ground carrying a lantern. They did not dare to venture any closer and quickly vacated the area.

Shadowy figures are said to dart about the headstones at night, moving far more quickly than a living human could and causing anyone visiting the cemetery to leave within minutes of arriving.

In my research, I had also read that Dabbs Cemetery was racially segregated and had been ever since it was established in the mid 1800s. I had never heard of this practice until I began traveling around the southern part of the United States. Apparently, it was fairly common to keep the African-American burial grounds separated from the Caucasian.

My journey to Dabbs Cemetery was an interesting one, as the directions I found were a little confusing. The cemetery was not in the middle of town; instead, it was reached by traveling unpaved back roads. The drive was gorgeous, and it was fun for my husband and me to travel off of the beaten path looking for this supposedly haunted graveyard.

As we pulled up, my attention was immediately drawn to the African-American side of the cemetery. The entrance was unmarked and there was nothing to indicate that anyone had been in that particular section to take care of the grounds in months, if not years. There was no gate; only a simple gravel entry from the road. I could not make any sense of the layout, as many of the headstones and grave markers were not arranged in any organized fashion. Some areas had no markers at all, though I suspect that graves are probably located in them. It made my heart ache to think that some people may not have had a proper burial at all, but were simply placed in the ground and forgotten.

The Caucasian side of the cemetery was easily viewable from the African-American side, but was sectioned off by a chain-link fence. The plots were neatly manicured, with flowers and trinkets placed at many of them. There was a large metal sign with the name of the cemetery adorning the gated entrance. A pavilion sat nearby with picnic tables available for visitors. The stark contrast between the two sides added to my sense of sadness.

As I wandered around the unkempt side of the cemetery in the daylight, I had the overwhelming feeling that Allen and I were not the only ones present. There wasn't anyone else around, but the area felt crowded to me. I routinely visit places known to have paranormal activity and I have become fairly used to the different sensations that can occur when I am in the presence of something unseen. I feel alerted, slightly more aware of my surroundings. It wasn't frightening at all, and I mentioned the feeling to Allen.

"Do we have a digital recorder with us?" I asked.

"We have one in the car. I'll go get it," he said.

Allen quickly returned with the recorder and switched it on. I knew it would be difficult to hear anything upon playback if there was much movement, so we kept still for awhile.

"My name is April and this is my husband, Allen," I said. "We thought we'd come out for a visit today. Is there anyone here with us that is willing to say hello?"

Neither of us heard anything out of the ordinary as we stood listening for a response. Upon playback of the recording, however, what sounds like a small girl's voice answers with an emphatic, "Hello!"

Less than five minutes into the recording, we also heard a male voice with a heavy southern drawl speaking.

"How y'all doing?" he asked.

A lot of people interested in researching the paranormal will often conduct sessions of recordings to review later for possible EVP capture. At times, I find it best to make statements and ask questions, pause, and then immediately play the recording back to see if I have obtained a response. This helps me to maintain a two-way conversation as best I can when someone is possibly trying to communicate with me. I imagine it must be frustrating for those on the other side to be engaged in a conversation and not have their statements or questions immediately acknowledged while we expect responses to our own. If you spoke to someone who refused to talk to you, you would most likely stop trying and walk away. I didn't want whoever was communicating with us to stop, and I was thrilled to hear them engaging us shortly after we started recording.

It is widely believed in the paranormal field that most phenomena occur in the nighttime hours, which has always baffled

Caucasian side of Dabbs Cemetery *(April Slaughter)*

me a bit. Most of us (though not all) tend to be busy and carry out our activities during the day and then rest and recharge our energy supply at night as we sleep. I am not sure it is all that different once we depart this life for the next, and assume that any hour of the day or night could prove to be a worthwhile time for investigating. Some of my best paranormal experiences have happened in the daylight hours, so it is difficult for me to believe that it is necessary to wait for nightfall before attempting to encounter interesting phenomena.

The African-American side of the cemetery, though poorly maintained, was quite serene and peaceful as I walked among the graves audibly inviting anyone who wanted to join to walk along with us and talk. Allen and I walked in different directions at one point, and he approached a section of graves that were heavily covered in brush and fallen trees.

"April, come over here for a minute and look at these markers," he said.

"Wow, I wouldn't have even known they were here if you hadn't found them," I said. "I thought this was just a patch of woods back here."

We stood quietly observing, and again we heard something interesting when we reviewed our recording. Several footsteps sounded as though they were quickly approaching the two of us. A soft voice muffled something we could not decipher and everything fell quiet. Nearly every time we paused to speak in hopes of a response in the cemetery, more footsteps were heard, and they certainly did not belong to either myself or Allen.

We decided that we should drive around to the cemetery entrance on the Caucasian side before heading out on the road. We spent about thirty minutes walking over the recently mown grass around the graves, but we were unable to hear or record anything while we were there. It had an entirely different feel to it, and not at all "crowded" like the other side had been.

I don't believe that every cemetery is haunted, as people are already dead when they arrive there. It has always seemed to me that they serve more as a place for the living to remember those they have loved and lost, rather than as magnets for ghosts. There isn't a doubt in my mind, however, that Allen and I were not the only individuals in the cemetery the afternoon of our visit to Dabbs. We had a ghostly visitor or two approach and engage us in conversation, even if only for brief moments at a time. Their footsteps and their voices are forever captured on our recording. It is my hope that on a visit in the very near future, I will not only be able to hear their voices again, but to see their faces and perhaps understand why they still walk the lonely landscape of Dabbs Cemetery.

CHAPTER 23

The Grove

JEFFERSON

The Grove exterior
(April Slaughter)

WHEN I FIRST MOVED TO TEXAS, I had no idea that I would discover some of the most amazing and interesting places that I had ever been. The state is home to nearly every type of landscape you can imagine. Whether you are looking for desert ghost towns, rolling hills covered in trees and wildflowers, or bustling downtown cities, you will find them in Texas. Some places have more ghostly lore associated with them than others, and Jefferson happens to be one of the most well-known.

Jefferson was originally established as a river port in east Texas where sternwheelers would travel with their cargo up the Mississippi River to the Red River, through Caddo Lake, and into Big Cypress Bayou. A massive log jam made it possible for steamboats to travel with their goods into Jefferson from New Orleans as the logs had dammed up the Red River, forming Caddo Lake and making Big Cypress a useful "turning basin."

Port cities were an invaluable asset to the economy as the railroad had not yet arrived in Texas and people greatly depended on the shipments brought in by the boats to survive and to cultivate their businesses. Captain William Perry arrived as one of the first settlers in Jefferson on a sternwheeler in 1844, and just four years later the town was incorporated.

Several families lived on the property that is now known as The Grove, but the home as it sits today was originally built by W. Frank Stilley and his wife Minerva in November 1861. Frank was a cotton broker, and Minerva's family owned and operated a cotton plantation in Marshall, making their marriage a highly beneficial business arrangement.

In 1866, a flood hit Jefferson and Frank's cotton brokering business was destroyed. In 1873, the log jam (nicknamed the "Great Raft") that enabled the sternwheelers to conduct their business in shipping to and from Jefferson was cleared out by the U.S. Army Corps of Engineers. The city was never the same. The steep fall in revenue took with it the growth and success that had once been so prevalent for the area. It is estimated that had Jefferson continued to grow as it had when it was first established, presently it would be the size of Houston.

In 1879, Minerva Stilley passed away. Charlie J. and Daphne Finch Young bought The Grove six years later. Charlie opened a barbershop in town and had many loyal, high-paying customers. He became a beloved member of the local community.

His wife Daphne planted and cultivated a beautiful garden, filled with orange day lilies and tiger lilies. She died in 1955 at the age of ninety-one, after having spent seventy years of her life at The Grove. Her funeral was held on the porch of the house so that she could be near the garden she loved before her burial.

Louise R. Young, Charlie and Daphne's daughter, was born in the home and spent nearly her entire ninety-six years there before her death in 1983. Patrick Hopkins bought the house in 1990 and opened it as The Grove Restaurant, naming the establishment after the nearly 140-year-old native Texas pecan trees that border it.

Current owners Mitchel and Tami Whitington acquired The Grove in 2002 and have delved into the history of everyone who lived on the property in hopes of preserving the information to share with future owners. They have also opened The Grove to public tours, providing guests with a colorful overview of Jefferson's history along with history of the home and past residents.

Mitchel Whitington is an author who has written about the paranormal phenomena that he, his wife, and their guests have continually experienced during their ownership of The Grove. My first introduction to the property came shortly after a friend of mine had gifted me a copy of Mitchel's books, *Ghosts of East Texas & the Pineywoods* and *A Ghost in My Suitcase: A Guide to Haunted Travel in America.*

The town of Jefferson is quite famous for its ghost stories, and I have spent a lot of time there over the past couple of years discovering as many of them as I could. The Grove captured my attention, and it was only a short time before I found myself contacting the Whitingtons to arrange a visit to their home.

Allen, Jerry Bowers, and I traveled to Jefferson one sunny Sunday afternoon, and arrived at The Grove as Mitchel took a small group of visitors through on a tour. He provided so much information on Jefferson and The Grove that I couldn't keep up on my note taking. Luckily, I had brought a digital recorder along, so all of the information would be available to me later upon playback of the audio.

"I am always asked at least two questions by our guests," Mitchel began. "First, I am asked if the house is truly haunted, to which I reply that yes, it is, but not in a Hollywood kind of way. Some people walk in and expect to see a scene straight out of the movie *Poltergeist*, but it just isn't like that.

"The second question I am asked is, being that it is indeed a haunted house, how in the world could my wife and I stand to live here? Well, just stick with me through the tour, and you'll see why by the time it comes to an end."

As we entered the house, we were directed to the main living room and parlor. It is in this room that many psychics and sensitives have felt the presence of a female spirit, standing close to a mirror that hangs on the wall near the corner. The name Rachel has been suggested to Mitchel as this spirit's name, but he hasn't found any hard evidence in the history of the house to validate that impression. Nevertheless, there is a woman who has been seen and spoken to, in this particular corner, especially when children visit.

Some curious enough to approach the house have reported that an older gentleman with a gun has literally run them off the property.

"He is our protective spirit," said Mitchel. "My wife and I don't believe that we'll ever see him, as he seems to trust us to take care of the place. However, he shows up often to others, and is described as looking just as solid as you or I." Who he is, and why he is so protective of The Grove is unclear.

As the tour moved to the dining room, Mitchel spoke about the three children born into the Young family—daughters Louise and Mable, and a son named James. Louise and Mable have a well-documented history, whereas James is much more of a mystery. The Whitingtons learned through the stories of an elderly local woman that James died at the age of twenty in the home, having committed suicide. He had hanged himself on the back porch in 1907. As was typical of the era, his situation was not openly discussed. Suicide meant that there was something terribly wrong in the family, so the details of James' life and death were mostly kept hidden. The entire Young family is buried together in one of the local cemeteries in Jefferson, with the exception of this young man. Mitchel and Tami have not been able to locate where his final resting place is.

I thought about James and wondered about his circumstances, hoping that he was finally in a place of peace and no longer troubled by whatever it was that had compelled him to take his own life. I found it endearing that Mitchel was sure to mention him on the tour, even though he did not personally believe that James was haunting the house.

Through The Grove's many transformations over the years, apparitions have become commonplace on the property. During a dinner theatre production held in the house one evening, a light technician was outside looking through a window when she was startled by a woman dressed in white standing on the east side of the house. As the technician approached the woman, she watched her walk toward the rear of the house. The lady in white stepped through the outside wall and instantly disappeared. At one point in time, there had been a door in the exact spot where the ghostly specter had been seen just before she vanished.

Less-detailed entities have also been sighted gliding through the garden. These figures appear to be more shadow-like and not identifiable as either male or female.

One interesting phenomenon consists of the inexplicable appearance of water in locations throughout the house. Sometimes it is seen as droplets on a particular mirror in the home, while on other occasions wet footprints have appeared on the floor as if someone had stepped out of a bath or puddle and walked through the home barefoot. No source for the water has been found, as the plumbing is in complete working order and the weather conditions on such days have been uneventful and dry.

The Whitingtons continue to experience a variety of unexplained events in their home, but insist that nothing has ever felt negative or threatening. Having been to the property myself, I can attest to the calm and peaceful atmosphere that it exudes. Mitchel and Tami are dedicated to preserving the story of The Grove and all who have previously called it home. It is obvious that they not only respect the history of property, but also the souls of those who are often seen, heard, and felt there.

Spotlight on Ghosts:
Lady in Blue

Texas has no shortage of interesting stories, but few are as bizarre as the mysterious "Lady in Blue." Her story begins as a young girl in seventeenth-century Spain, in a convent—her home—that she would never physically leave during her sixty-three years. María Jesus de Ágreda was a devout Spanish nun who dedicated her life to the Catholic faith. She would become a legend in areas of Arizona, New Mexico, and Texas without ever stepping foot outside of her country, or her own hometown.

At the age of eighteen, Maria experienced the first of what would become many mystical transitions from the physical world into the spiritual. One day during prayer in the convent, Maria reportedly went into a trance-like state. A beggar who had come to the convent to pray witnessed the event and reported that a blue light suddenly enveloped the young nun as she knelt. The light was said to have lifted her several feet above the floor as she remained unmoving and seemingly still in prayer.

As time went on, Maria began to experience these trances during her daily routine. She said that she was blessed with visions in which she saw dark-colored people in the wilderness of the southwestern United States. She said she often spoke with them and shared her faith with them in hopes that they would seek out the word of God. It is believed she made over five hundred of these visits in a process known as bi-location, teleportation, or astral projection—the ability to physically be in one place and spiritually in another at the same time.

Maria would often visit the Jumano Indian people of Texas, which resulted in their desire to receive instruction in the Catholic faith. During her visitations, it is said that she came to them speaking their native tongue, though she had never learned their language. When asked about this peculiarity, she said that she simply traveled to deliver a message and God provided her a way to communicate with the Indians. Five years after her death in 1665, a book she authored titled *The Mystical City of God* was published. It outlined her extraordinary views and experiences and is said to be one of the most controversial texts in the history of the church.

Throughout the recent centuries, many people have often reported seeing the spirit of the Lady in Blue visit them in times of need, sickness, or desperation. It is reported that she appeared in Sabinetown in the 1840s to care for those afflicted by a "black tongue" epidemic, suddenly disappearing when the illness was finally under control. Her legend lives on in southwestern Texas, where many believe she is constantly watching over them, still performing in death the work she loved in life.

CHAPTER 24

Ghost Train of Jefferson

JEFFERSON

Ghost Train of Jefferson train depot
(Jerry Bowers)

NEARLY EVERY NOOK AND CRANNY in the city of Jefferson, Texas, is said to be haunted. Locals not only expect ghosthunters to visit, they cater to them. Haunted hotels, coffee shops, restaurants, and several "ghost walk" tours lure hundreds of paranormal enthusiasts into town every year. My first visit to Jefferson was no different; looking for ghosts is something I consider my full-time job. I was told that the once-thriving river port town had plenty of phenomena for me to discover, and I had only lived in Texas a matter of days before I was pestering my husband to take me to Jefferson.

Allen and I did all of the typical tourist stuff, stopping in to the little antique shops and even taking a ride on a horse-drawn carriage as we toured the historic streets and neighborhoods. Although it was fall when we visited, the heat and humidity of summer had not yet left Texas. We met up with a small group of people in the early afternoon to investigate a covered rail car that sat just beyond the Historic Jefferson Railway Train Depot in the woods of the Big Cypress Bayou.

I knew nothing of the rail car's history, going in only with the knowledge that people had claimed it was haunted. We split into small groups and each took turns inside the car with their cameras, digital recorders, and various other devices, hoping to catch something paranormal.

When it was our turn, Allen decided to test out the K-II meter while I ran video. It was daytime, but from inside the passenger car you could barely tell. The windows were nearly all covered over and only a random streak of light or two found its way in. Allen sat on one of the passenger seats with the K-II and began to ask a series of questions. Nothing happened at first, but then I noticed something odd happening with the video camera. As I was looking into the viewfinder, the picture would become increasingly blurry when it had just been crystal clear. Every few seconds, the camera would focus and then blur again.

"The camera is acting strange," I said to Allen.

"What's it doing?" he asked.

"I can't get it to stay focused."

Immediately after we noted the strange incident, the lights on the K-II meter in Allen's hand went berserk. A long beam of light passed underneath his hand and under one of the other passenger seats. The beam moved toward the other side of the rail car, then back toward us, and the camera refused to stay focused until the anomaly faded away. The lights on the K-II had reacted every time the light passed by it, but they never lit up again after that. Something in the car had triggered the EMF sensor in the K-II and made my camera act strangely, but we had no idea what it was. We waited several more minutes before deciding to let the next small group of people take our place in the car.

We gathered our things and stepped outside to see that the others were all standing with their backs to the rail car. Jerry Bowers turned to look at us and was pointing his finger out towards the woods nearby. He motioned to us to come closer.

"Can y'all hear that?" he asked.

We stood still for a few moments listening for whatever it was that had caught Jerry's attention. All of a sudden, I heard what sounded like a man yelling off in the distance. My first thought was that someone was out there and possibly needed help.

"We need to go out there," said Allen.

"Let's go," I replied, and off the two of us went out into the woods beyond the train tracks.

We wandered around for about ten minutes, and never heard the yelling again. We didn't even know which direction we were headed. All of a sudden, Allen stood still and looked down at the ground. At his feet was a peculiar glass bottle. He bent down and picked it up, and for reasons neither of us ever figured out, we brought it home with us. It sits in our kitchen window. Several weeks after we brought it home, a psychic friend of ours told us that the bottle was the reason Allen felt drawn into the woods, and that the spirit of a woman was attached to it. We were told she was friendly, so it didn't bother us that we had brought a "stranger" home.

The time came to head back to the train depot for a ride through the reportedly haunted woods. I was more than just a little relieved when the sun finally set and the air cooled off just enough to sustain what little energy I had left. Allen, Jerry, and I sat in the last seat at the back of the train. A switchman was the only person behind us, as his job was to jump off of the back during the ride to switch the rails.

While the train slowly moved along the tracks, a guide at the front of the passenger car relayed stories of what others had experienced on the ride and in the woods that surrounded us. It was completely dark outside, and it was difficult to see any further than a few inches out from the car without turning on a flashlight.

The switchman behind us jumped off the train and disappeared. A short while later, a loud thud hit the back of the car and the three of us just assumed he had caught up and jumped back on. I turned to look, but no one was there.

"Someone's behind the train," said Jerry.

"I know, I can hear them talking," I replied.

We could hear what sounded like a quickly spoken conversation directly behind the train car. Jerry snapped a couple of photographs, but they turned out to be completely black. I grabbed my flashlight and shined it out on the tracks just behind the rail car. About ten feet off of to the right, I saw a man standing next to a tree. A split second later, he was gone. He hadn't moved; I didn't see him walk away. He was just gone. I shined the light directly out where I had seen him standing, but he was no longer there.

"Did you see him?" I asked Allen and Jerry.

"Who?" they asked.

"The guy by the tree out there."

Neither of them had seen the man, and the others on the train didn't report anything out of the ordinary when we pulled back up to the depot. I asked the guide who the individual might have been, but he said that no one else should have been out there. I wondered if the specter had anything to do with the conversation Jerry and I had heard carrying on just behind us as the train slowly crept along the tracks.

The depot itself also had reported paranormal phenomena, so we all wanted to check it out before concluding our efforts that night. Destry Brown, vice president of operations at the Jefferson Railway, spoke to me about some of the things he had experienced since he started working there in April 2002.

"I spend most of my time here in the depot, and there is always something going on in here," he said. "We have a string of sleigh bells that hang on our door, and at any given time they will ring as if someone had ahold of them, shaking them violently, but no one is there.

"When I am all alone in the building," he continued, "I'll be working on something in the upstairs lobby and hear the office doors downstairs opening and closing. It's really strange because a lot of things happen when I have the building locked up tight with the alarm set. No one else could be in the building without my knowing it."

"Has anything else happened when you were here alone?" I asked.

"We have a toy box upstairs with several small cars in it for kids to play with while they wait for the train. One night, I had everything locked up and was working in my office downstairs when I distinctly heard what sounded like those toy cars rolling across the floor upstairs. I went upstairs to see what was going on, but the cars were right where they should be in the toy box."

"Why do you think the depot is haunted?" I asked.

"I think the location is more haunted than the actual structure," said Destry. "This was all an industrial area during the 1850s, and I know there were probably a number of accidents here. Also, passengers coming in on the steamboats sometimes had to walk into Jefferson from about four miles downriver if the boats couldn't make it all the way up. It wasn't the safest area, and I am sure many of them were mugged or hurt as they tried to make it into town."

With the area's rich history, there really was no telling just who might be haunting the Historic Jefferson Railway and depot building.

When our small group tried to catch something paranormal on our audio and video equipment, we were disappointed that nothing out of the ordinary happened. I've learned that a lot of ghosthunting is playing the "hurry-up-and-wait" game. Nothing is ever predictable, and having patience can often be difficult.

Late that night, just as we were packing up our equipment to leave, Jerry picked up his digital voice recorder that had been sitting on the counter. He had almost forgotten it was there. Had he left it behind, he may never have discovered what he had captured when he returned home and reviewed the audio.

At the very end of the recording, when all was quiet and we were about to leave, a voice made a simple and humorous observation.

"Tourists!"

CHAPTER 25

Scottsville Cemetery
SCOTTSVILLE

The "angel that moves" memorial at Scottsville Cemetery
(*Jerry Bowers*)

SEVERAL YEARS AGO, a friend of mine turned me on to an HBO series called *Six Feet Under*. The show centers around the Fishers—a family of undertakers that live in and operate a funeral home in Los Angeles, California. The series began with the tragic death of Nathaniel Fisher, the family patriarch and owner of the Fisher & Sons Funeral Home. His hearse was broadsided by a bus while he was on his way to the airport to pick up his oldest son on Christmas Eve.

As his casket is being lowered into the ground during the graveside service, the scene cuts to Nathaniel sitting on top of the hearse parked nearby, witnessing his own funeral. He looks on unconcerned, wearing an Hawaiian aloha shirt and sipping a tropical drink from a coconut. From that scene on, I was hooked on the show, as it reassured me that I wasn't the only one who wondered if I might be able to attend my own funeral. How would I perceive the process? What would my reaction to it be? Every time I step foot in a cemetery, I look around at all of the plots and am instantly empathetic for the families and friends who have had to endure the death of a loved one. I have been to my share of funerals and have acquired a deep respect for the different rituals we all use to honor those we have lost. I am especially intrigued with the individualized stones and monuments that are erected in remembrance of those that have passed.

Scottsville Cemetery is home to some of the most beautiful funerary statues I have ever seen. Looking at pictures online did not sate me, and on a beautiful Saturday afternoon when most other wives would be bugging their husbands to take them shopping, I was begging mine to take me to a cemetery—and a reportedly haunted one at that!

Scottsville Cemetery isn't very large, but the stories that have come out of it sure are! In almost every cemetery, you will find statues of angels. They symbolize a belief in the divine, a higher power, and peace—ideals that bring comfort to the living and honor the dead. There is, however, one angel in Scottsville Cemetery that has caused a great deal of fright in those lurking about in the dark.

An account I found online detailed an incident where six individuals had driven out to the cemetery to spend some time on the grounds at night. As they walked around with their flashlights, nothing much was happening and they were all a bit disappointed. They decided to leave and began to walk toward their car when they passed one monument that sent a jolt of fear through them. The beautiful life-sized angel draped over one of the headstones they had seen when they arrived had vanished! All six people knew she had been there earlier, but where was she now? Had she flown up into the night sky, or was she lurking somewhere among the other headstones? Neither idea was very comforting. The group ran for their car and drove quickly away.

This particular angel has scared quite a few others as well. Some say if you stand close to her for any long period of time at night, she will lift her head to look you right in the eye. Naturally skeptical that such a large piece of stone could become animated and interact with people, I wanted to see her face-to-face.

Allen and lead investigator with The Paranormal Source, Jerry Bowers, accompanied me on my excursion to Scottsville, just as eager as I was to see the mysterious angel step down from her place atop someone's grave and move as she had been reported to do. We arrived in the late afternoon and immediately took notice of the angel. There she sat, perfectly carved and lifelike, seemingly weeping over a headstone. If she moved during the couple of hours we spent on the grounds, she must have done it while we weren't paying attention. Nevertheless, I kept looking back in her direction just to make sure she stayed put. She did.

At the west side of the cemetery there is a springhouse at the bottom of a hill, and just beyond it is a peculiar set of stairs ascending a hill to empty space. It is said that at one time a large two-story home sat on that hill, but it had burned to the ground sometime over fifty years ago. Before it was destroyed, locals reported that they would stand on those steps looking up at the house and hear sounds coming from within. Disembodied conversations and the sound of someone dragging furniture across the floor fascinated and frightened many. They knew the house was empty, so who or what was still in there?

Now that the house is gone, you'd think that the strange phenomena would have left with it, right? Wrong. Curious kids, regular cemetery visitors, and paranormal investigators have all said that as they stand at the top of the stairs, they have heard a woman weeping down near the springhouse just below them. Sometimes the sound is faint, while at others it sounds as though a living, breathing person is obviously distraught.

I wanted to test this out, so just as the sun was setting for the evening, I climbed the stairs and sat at the top of the hill. Allen and Jerry were off in another corner of the cemetery, quietly discussing different headstones and markers. I hadn't felt anything odd since we arrived, so I saw no problem with sitting by myself as the sun slowly disappeared.

I turned my digital recorder on, but within seconds, it turned itself off. I checked the batteries, and they were not drained. They had just been replaced an hour or so earlier. Not thinking much of it, I switched the recorder on again. Ten or fifteen seconds passed and off it went again. The power to the recorder was not going to stay on. I abandoned the idea of recording any audio, and just sat there in silence.

Nothing out of the ordinary was happening—that is, until Allen and Jerry came into view walking toward the steps. A short, shrill sound quickly came and went. I put my hand out to signal to Allen and Jerry to stop where they were and not to come any closer. I slowly reached for the recorder sitting next to me on the ground, and tried turning it on again. It still refused to work. Jerry took a few photographs of me on the steps, but he saw nothing out of the ordinary in them.

Several minutes passed with the three of us being still as it got darker and darker by the second. I locked eyes with Allen as soon as I began hearing something again. This time, it was unmistakable. Someone was crying, and they sounded awfully close to me. I couldn't tell if it was a woman or a child, as they can often sound very similar, but I knew without a doubt that I was not hearing an animal or something in the distance I could have mistaken for a human cry. My heart sank, but I did not move. A soft sobbing seemed to come closer and closer to me. It was only a matter of sixty seconds or so, and all was silent again.

I waited for a moment or two, and slowly got up to walk back down the stairs to where Allen and Jerry were standing.

"You heard that, right?" I asked them.

"Yeah, we heard it all right. It sounded like it was closer to you than it was to us," said Allen.

"Was it a child, do you think?" asked Jerry.

"I don't know," I answered. "Whoever or whatever it was made my heart hurt with that cry, though. It sounded so mournful."

Allen and Jerry wanted to see if the incident would repeat itself if I stayed near the bottom of the stairs as they sat at the top of them. I sat on the ground next to the springhouse and the two of them sat where I had just been. None of us spoke and we kept as still as we could. About fifteen minutes passed by uneventfully. Suddenly, I felt as though someone was walking toward me and I instinctively looked to my right to see who it was. No one was there, but a quiet voice clearly said, "Hello." I quickly sat up straight and looked around. Allen and Jerry were looking right at me as I pointed to my right, signaling to them that something was there. Allen shrugged his shoulders. He hadn't heard the voice saying hello, and neither had Jerry.

They stood up and descended the steps. I sat still.

"What happened?" asked Allen.

"Someone said hello to me," I said.

"Did you hear anything else?" asked Jerry.

"No. Just hello, but it was as if someone were standing within a foot of me," I replied.

I handed the digital recorder to Allen and asked him to take a look at it because it seemed to be malfunctioning. He turned it on and hit record.

"Seems to be working fine now," he said.

"Of course it is working *now*!" I replied. "Just after I really *needed* it to work!"

Stairs leading to nowhere at Scottsville Cemetery *(Jerry Bowers)*

The daylight would be completely gone at any moment, so we decided it was time to head home. We did not have permission to be on the grounds after dark.

We passed the monument with the infamous moving angel and I waved goodbye.

"Next time angel . . . it's your turn."

Spotlight on Ghosts:
Stampede Mesa

Cattle ranchers once considered this hilltop in Crosby, Texas, which overlooks the White River, an ideal place to rest and feed their herds as they drove them across the plains. What is known today as Stampede Mesa provided a good source of water and a useful view of the surrounding area to warn the men of any approaching trouble. The men and their animals could rest and refuel before continuing on with their journey.

In the fall of 1889, a trail boss reportedly ordered his men to drive his cattle to the mesa. In so doing, they unknowingly cut through a local farmer's land, inadvertently acquiring a few of his animals along with their own. When the farmer realized what had happened, he rode up to the mesa and demanded the immediate return of his cattle, which he was granted. The farmer began to round up his animals, but he also attempted to steal a few belonging to the herd on the mesa. An argument ensued. The overworked and exhausted cowboys demanded the farmer to return to his land empty-handed and revisit the mesa the next morning to resolve the issue.

The farmer did return, but long before the sun rose the next morning. In the middle of the night, the cattle on the mesa began to stampede and the cowboys watching over them tried to round them up as they headed toward the steepest ledge. Several head of cattle were lost, driven over the edge to their deaths. Witnesses accused the bitter farmer of returning in the night to force the cattle off the cliff.

Infuriated by the loss of so many animals, the trail boss believed he had the right to exact his own version of justice. His men forced the farmer back to the mesa, bound and blindfolded. He was placed on his likewise blindfolded horse and driven off the mesa just as the helpless cattle had been the night before. No one was dispatched to fetch and bury the farmer. He was left to lie with the animals he was accused of killing in the stampede.

Ever since that fateful day, legend has it that the doomed farmer is still often seen bound to his horse headed for the cliff. Cattlemen became afraid to rest their herds at Stampede Mesa, as it was rumored that the angry farmer was still seeking justice and would drive their cattle to the same fate as those before them. Campers and travelers staying in the area have often been startled awake in the middle of the night by the sound of a massive stampede of animals that simply are not there.

CHAPTER 26

Spaghetti Warehouse
HOUSTON

**Spaghetti Warehouse exterior
(Pete Haviland)**

IT HAS BEEN NEARLY A DECADE since I made my first visit to Texas. I was overwhelmed with the vastness of the state, the pride of those who called it home, and of course, food like I had never tasted before in my life. On that very first trip out, I learned that Texas would never let me down when it came to finding something new and fun to experience. I distinctly remember stopping to have dinner at the Spaghetti Warehouse in Dallas, and I loved it. Now that I am a Texas resident, you'd think the nostalgia would have long worn off—but it hasn't.

My husband Allen, a Texas native, has lived in almost every area of the state at one time or another, and when I began looking for haunted places to research for the book, he suggested I look into the Spaghetti Warehouse in Houston.

"I thought that was in Dallas," I said.

"They have a few of them in Texas, but I know the one in

Houston is supposedly haunted," he replied.

I looked it up, and he was right. The Spaghetti Warehouse in Houston did indeed have several ghost stories attached to it, but as with any other place, I wasn't going to be convinced until I could visit and get a feel for it myself. Allen and I made arrangements to visit some of his family in the Houston area and put the restaurant on our list of places to stop for a bite.

The building that now houses the restaurant was originally constructed in the early 1900s as the Desel-Boettcher Warehouse, and it has served many functions over the past century. Produce, storage, cotton, and pharmaceutical businesses came and went until the building was purchased in the 1970s and renovated into the Spaghetti Warehouse restaurant. Some say that early on in the building's history, several workers suffered unfortunate accidents that caused their deaths.

One story is particularly heartbreaking. A woman whose husband worked at the warehouse was cooking dinner and waiting for him to return home from work. He did not arrive at his usual time, and she started to worry. It was not like him to be late. A short time passed, and as she was pacing the house, she heard the front door open and the sound of footsteps coming down the hall. Out of the corner of her eye, she saw a figure quickly pass by. Thinking her husband had finally returned home, she called out to him but he did not respond. After searching the home frantically for her husband in vain, the woman ran to the warehouse only to find that her husband had fallen to his death in the warehouse's elevator shaft. As the story goes, the widow was found dead in her home on the first-year anniversary of her husband's death. No cause of death was ever determined, but most believed she had died of a broken heart.

For years, restaurant employees have reported seeing the apparition of a woman in a long white dress on the second floor, and speculate that it is the ghost of the widow haunting the building that claimed her husband's life.

Did customers see the widow's apparition too? I didn't know, but I was hoping I would when we arrived at the restaurant for dinner one evening. The restaurant is gorgeously decorated with antiques, including a chandelier from New York's Penn Station, a trolley car, and a hand-carved staircase removed from one of England's castles. It didn't look at all like the Spaghetti Warehouse I had visited in Dallas, but it had the same warmth and energy about it. I was more interested in the décor than the meal, but I ended up enjoying both a great deal. The restaurant was packed, and I didn't have a whole lot of time to peruse as much of it as I would have liked, but it fascinated me enough to try and dig a little deeper into its haunted history.

As soon as we made it back home, I contacted Pete Haviland of Lone Star Spirits in Houston and asked him if he'd had any knowledge or experience with the Spaghetti Warehouse.

"Yes, my team and I have investigated the restaurant many times," Pete replied. "Every time I do any work there, I get pulled aside and told the latest experience. The stories are fascinating."

"What sorts of things have happened in the restaurant?" I asked.

"Over the years, many people have reported seeing the apparition of a woman in white on the upstairs floor," he began. "Dishwashers have even reported looking up through the window in front of their work station and seeing a white, sullen face of a woman looking directly at them."

Pete went on to tell me that several instances of activity seemed to center around the kitchen area.

"During one renovation, a carpenter was working near the kitchen. When he began working, the dining room had been neat and tidy—nothing out of the ordinary. Well, when he took a moment to look around again, the dining room chairs had somehow been stacked three high! He quit working in the restaurant after that, and never came back.

"Waiters and waitresses have often complained of being tripped as they walked out of the kitchen to serve food to their customers."

On one occasion, arguing was heard coming from the kitchen. Plates were being broken and a knife had even been thrown, all without any visible explanation.

"What have you personally experienced during your investigations?" I asked.

"Directly above the entrance to the building, there is a small dining room that sits where the old elevator used to be. I have personally witnessed the apparition of a little girl in that room, as did others who were with me during an overnight investigation. We heard the sounds of children laughing and a male-sounding moan."

I asked Pete why he thought the spirits of children might be haunting the restaurant.

"There is an urn cabinet upstairs that is rumored to have once housed the cremated remains of orphaned children," Pete explained. "A medium I worked with told me that she believed the spirit of the little girl I had seen was attached to that cabinet, as she had somehow gotten herself locked in the bottom portion of it during a game of hide-and-seek and had suffocated. Several people have also said they've heard children crying in the vicinity of the cabinet.

"Investigator Tom Kennedy saw the apparition of a man in a wool suit in the small dining room above the entrance just seconds before a medium described the spirit to a separate room of people. Tom hadn't been with them, but both he and the medium reported identical descriptions of the man."

"Has anything strange happened anywhere else in the building?" I asked.

"Team member Rebecca Draper conducted an experiment in the basement where she placed a small rubber ball in front of her on the floor, and asked that someone move it so she could see," said Pete. "The ball did indeed move, and a rather significant distance. Unexplained footsteps were heard in the basement as well, and we also received reports that someone saw what they described as a young slave cowering in one of the corners down there."

"I have heard that the staircase in the restaurant is active as well," I said.

"Yes. People have reported seeing a man tumbling down the stairs. Two separate mediums I have spoken with tell me that they see a man with heart issues, possibly causing a heart attack and a fall down the stairs."

I asked Pete his opinion of why he thought the Spaghetti Warehouse was haunted.

"I think there are many factors to it," he answered. "The building has been home to many businesses over the years, and there are many stories about people having been involved in fatal accidents. The restaurant is also filled with antiques that could have brought with them their own residual energy. Those sorts of things can really add up and cause people to experience phenomena on a rather consistent basis."

Pete and his team at Lone Star Spirits continue their ongoing research of the historical warehouse building. They hope to determine whether or not the phenomena experienced there are genuine manifestations of an intelligent and interactive spirit (or spirits), purely residual energy, or perhaps even poltergeist activity.

Researchers have long been examining the possibility that poltergeists are the manifestations of the human mind's ability to project outward into the physical environment, causing chaotic movements of objects and often mirroring things we believe to be paranormal in nature.

Allen and I truly enjoyed the unique dining experience of the Spaghetti Warehouse and the many stories of the ghosts that call it home. I didn't want to leave, and felt sad that I lived so far away that I couldn't just pop in from time to time.

If there are ghosts haunting the restaurant who are content and at peace to be there, I hope I have the opportunity to see and interact with them on a future visit. It is my sincere hope that the forlorn "lady in white" will someday be able to let go of the past that binds her to the old warehouse building and reunite with the spirit of her beloved husband.

Lone Star Spirits and The Paranormal Source, Inc. plan a collaborative effort to investigate the restaurant in the coming months. I hope we will be able to shed a bit more light on that which tends to stay hidden in the dark.

CHAPTER 27

USS *Texas*
La Porte

**USS *Texas*
exterior
(Jerry Bowers)**

WHEN I WAS A LITTLE GIRL, one of my all-time favorite board games was Battleship. Naturally, I was usually the one who lost, but I still had a great time trying to sink my opponent's fleet. If you think about it, it's strange that a popular board game for children was inspired by vessels of destruction. I suppose G.I. Joe or the myriad of other aggressive games and toys available to youngsters today aren't much better. At any rate, I have fond memories of the game, and have always thought that an actual real-life battleship would be one of the coolest things to see.

The battleship USS *Texas* rests today at the San Jacinto Battleground a short distance from Houston. The ship spent thirty-four years and six weeks as a U.S. Navy vessel, commissioned in 1914 and decommissioned in 1948. The "Mighty T" sailed 728,000 miles during its service, and it is the only remaining

United States Navy battleship that fought in both World Wars. It has undergone quite a few renovations, but much of the ship remains as it was when it first launched into open waters.

For years, visitors to the ship have reported seeing the apparition of a red-headed sailor in his dress whites smiling at them as they pass by. He is sometimes seen standing near a ladder or walking along the ship's deck, and has earned the appropriate nickname of "Red." Those who have tried to approach the sailor and say hello are often disappointed at his lack of a response shortly before he turns a corner and disappears. He never speaks, but the smile on his face would indicate that he is happy being aboard the ship.

I became a Navy wife shortly after I turned twenty, and my first husband was often deployed on several different types of Navy ships during his time in the military. My first opportunity to walk onboard a Navy vessel was on a different type of ship called a frigate. In the past decade, I have been on all types of Navy vessels, and they are not exactly the homiest of environments. Our men and women in the service spend large amounts of time on these ships (some of them likened to floating cities), and none of them were built for comfort.

There's no telling the exact number of sailors who lived and worked on the *Texas*. Although living on these ships and spending so much time away from family and friends is difficult, sailors are incredibly dedicated people and it is not surprising to me that their spirits are believed to walk the narrow hallways of this battleship to this day.

When I first compiled my list of locations for my haunted road trip, my husband was excited to see the battleship *Texas* listed as a destination.

"I haven't been to the ship since I was a kid, but I'd made many trips out there when my family was living in Houston," said Allen.

When Allen and I arrived at the *Texas* and climbed aboard, I was only half-serious when I asked him if he'd ever seen a ghost aboard the ship.

"Come to think of it, I think I actually may have," he said. "One summer we'd had family come out to Houston to visit us, and whenever we had family come out, visiting the *Texas* was just something we did.

"I don't ever remember hearing that the ship was haunted when I was a kid, so I didn't visit thinking I would run into anything strange while I was there."

"How old were you when you had a strange experience here?" I asked.

"Thirteen or fourteen, maybe. I can't remember exactly."

Allen pointed out the enormous gun barrels jutting out toward the front of the ship as we walked along the top deck.

"On this particular visit, I wanted to crawl up into one of the main turrets that housed one of these fourteen-inch guns," he continued. "No one else wanted to crawl up in there with me because they knew it was going to be extremely hot in there. It's an entirely enclosed space, and on a hot summer day it wouldn't be fun in there for long.

"I decided I wanted to go up inside anyway, so I crawled up the ladder. When I got into the turret area, there was an older gentleman sitting on a small steel seat inside. I said hello, and just started looking around at everything. I was in awe of how much stuff had been crammed into such a small space, and I made mention of how large the gun was.

"That apparently sparked his interest, and he told me that the very spot we were standing in was his duty station during World War II. His entire naval career was spent manning that gun, and as I asked questions about the various controls and whatnot in the room, he calmly explained to me how each and every one of them worked.

"He told me how hot it would get in that room, and his only reprieve from the heat would be when he stripped down to his underwear to keep as cool as possible. These guns were not automatic. They'd shoot one huge round and then have to be reloaded. It was seriously hard work to keep that gun firing when it needed to be."

"I wonder how it felt for him to be back in that space," I said.

"He had a very solemn but peaceful look on his face during our entire conversation," said Allen. "I could tell that he was proud of the time he spent there, but he also looked very worn by the experience."

"I got distracted by something and for a short moment my attention was pulled away from him," Allen continued. "I turned back toward him to ask about something, but he was gone."

"Gone? You mean he just up and left the room?" I asked.

"Yes, but I didn't hear or see him leave. He just wasn't there anymore."

Allen did not suspect that he might have carried on a conversation with a ghost. He had no idea the ship was reportedly haunted. He was just interested in seeing the mechanics of it. When he crawled out of the turret, he mentioned the man to his family but none of them had seen him. He continued with his tour of the ship, and didn't think much more of the incident until now.

"I wonder if you interrupted the spirit of a sailor stopping in for a visit to his old duty station," I said.

"I don't know. He was there one second, and the next he was gone. He was an older guy, so it's not as if he could have just taken off that quickly without my noticing."

As ghosthunters, I think we tend to forget that not everything works according to our timeline, or in the way we would most like them to. We're preoccupied during the day with our lives and the things we need to get done, but how often do we stop to think that perhaps those on the other side have schedules or routines as well? We want ghosts to give us signs of their presence when we're lurking about in some dark place, not necessarily when they want to give them to us.

It's something I have thought about for years—how often are we seeing and experiencing the spirits of those who have passed on during our regular, everyday lives and not realizing it? It is possible that Allen met and spoke with an individual who had died years earlier, but because he seemed real and physical at the time (and appeared in the middle of the day), Allen automatically perceived him as a living, breathing person. I truly believe that the dead are all around us, and that seeing and interacting with them is not exclusive to those with psychic abilities.

I don't think that every ghost we encounter is "earth bound." In fact, I think spirits often make nostalgic visits of their own to people and places that meant a great deal to them during their lives. I don't presume to know for sure, but part of me thinks the sailor Allen encountered probably lived a long and happy life once he left the *Texas*. He may have died somewhere else in the country, or on the opposite side of the planet, but this ship probably meant enough to him to revisit it.

Sailor after sailor came and went on the battleship *Texas*. They saw times of peace as well as times of war. They suffered through being separated from their families, working long, hard hours, and probably endured rather frightening moments on numerous occasions. The entire spectrum of human emotion, from devastation and loss to victory and elation, was experienced on this ship. Is it any wonder that a sailor or two might still be "manning the rails" long after the battleship's days at sea have ended?

Spotlight on Ghosts:
Ghost Dogs of Orozimbo Plantation

The Battle of San Jacinto occurred on April 21, 1836, and lasted a mere eighteen minutes. Sam Houston led the Texas army to fight Santa Anna, the president of Mexico, resulting in the loss of hundreds of men, only nine of which were Texas soldiers. San Jacinto was the victory that ended the Texas Revolution and secured Texas' independence from Mexico. Santa Anna was caught dressed as a common soldier the day after the battle, and he was held prisoner at several plantations in the south while his captors negotiated his fate. He was eventually transported to the Orozimbo Plantation on the Brazos River, less than a dozen miles north of West Columbia.

A Mexican officer accompanied by several of his men made plans to advance on the plantation and free their president. The thick trees bordering the river provided an excellent cover as they advanced one stormy evening, taking advantage of the sound of the pouring rain to conceal their approach to the farmhouse in which Santa Anna was held prisoner. Just as they were about to rush the guards, an eerie and unmistakable sound of howling dogs came quickly towards them, and the Mexican men were forced to retreat. Those keeping guard at the farmhouse went to investigate, but found no animals in the area.

The howling dogs had been heard by many, yet no one could explain where they had come from as they had not been seen. Speculation arose that they may have belonged to a man who went off to war and never came home, forever leaving his faithful friends to search for him.

It has been well over a century since Santa Anna was held at Orozimbo, yet stories of the phantom dogs never seem to fade away. In fact, many people still claim to hear the pack roaming through the dense jungle of trees near the property, letting out an eerie howl as they approach. While Santa Anna was eventually allowed to return to his country, the ghosts dogs are still—and might forever be—keeping watch over Orozimbo Plantation.

South Texas

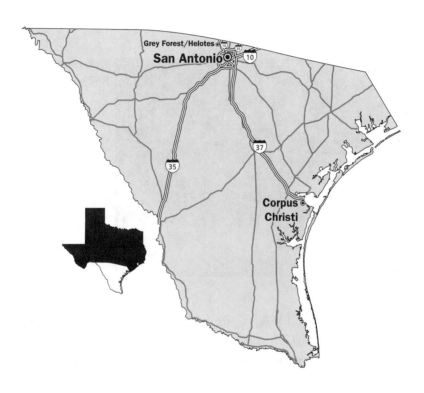

Corpus Christi
USS *Lexington*

Grey Forest/Helotes
Grey Moss Inn

San Antonio
The Alamo

CHAPTER 28

Grey Moss Inn
GREY FOREST / HELOTES

Patio seating at the Grey Moss Inn restaurant (River Rock Photography)

FOR TWENTY-THREE YEARS, Nell Baeten has known there are ghosts in her restaurant.

"I have never set out to convince anyone that there are spirits here, and I never will," she said. "Strange things happen all the time and the spirits here have become part of my life. Fact is, it's my job to run the restaurant, not to try and make anyone else believe it is haunted."

That was how my conversation with Nell began when I made my first trip out to the Grey Moss Inn and expressed my desire to include it in a book about Texas haunts. Several of my friends had dined at the restaurant over the years, and had suggested to me that it had a resident ghost or two.

Anyone can claim to have ghosts, and I have found it is not at all uncommon for places of business to conveniently become "haunted." Let's face it—ghosts are intriguing, and have the potential of drawing in a crowd. It's a great marketing tool if you can pull it off, and I have seen it happen often. What impressed me most about Nell and the Grey Moss Inn is that she acknowledges that the resident ghosts are there but doesn't use them to attract customers.

Texas is big state, and I had scores of locations I could have chosen to include in this book, but in the end, I wanted to bring attention to the places I most believed in. The Grey Moss Inn is one such place. The restaurant is well-known for its delectable menu and impeccable customer service, and not so much for its ghosts, but the more I got to know about the paranormal goings on there, I couldn't pass up the opportunity to visit and share its story.

The restaurant was built just outside of Grey Forest, Texas, in 1929 and was originally run by Mary Howell. She lived in a small cottage on the property and took great pride in serving her customers. Up until recently, little had changed in the main dining room of the restaurant over the years except for the occasional change in paint color. In early 2009, the Baetens decided it was time for a bit of an overhaul and hired contractors to remodel the restaurant.

"I knew before we even started on it that the spirits here would be disturbed," said Nell. "I didn't mention it to any of the men that came in to work on the remodel, but I wasn't at all surprised when they mentioned they had seen things in the restaurant."

"What did they see?" I asked.

"There were three or four guys sanding down some of the wood who said they saw several different people moving around as they worked. They also caught sight of a woman in the garden room who just up and disappeared."

The contractors also noticed several people they had not seen before wandering around the restaurant, as if they were busy working on their own tasks. As soon as their attention was drawn to them they were no longer there.

"Is this place haunted?" they asked Nell.

As soon as the dining room renovation was completed, Nell began putting up her own personal touches on the walls and shelves.

"I had a beautiful plate I wanted to display on one of the shelves. It didn't exactly go with the room's décor, but I really liked it," she said. "It was red and had these beautiful gold foil streaks running through it. As soon as I put it up on the shelf and made sure it was secure, I thought to myself, *I wonder how the spirits will like this plate, as it's so different.*"

Just as the thought crossed Nell's mind, the plate began to fall forward. She quickly reacted to grab it, but it toppled over the back of her hands and smashed to pieces on the floor.

"I guess they answered *that* question," she remarked.

"How do the employees feel about your ghostly residents?" I asked her.

"Well, one of our servers was spooked a little one night," Nell answered. "At the end of the day, he would walk around the restaurant to make sure everything was shut down and locked for the night before leaving. On this particular night, as he walked to the office area, he glanced back in the direction of the main dining room and noticed there was a light on. He knew he had just turned that light out moments earlier. As he walked back in to turn it off, he reached for the switch and glanced across the adjacent dining room, where he saw a face staring back at him. He moved slowly and watched as the face mirrored his movements exactly."

"Was he seeing his own reflection in something?" I asked.

"He said the man looked nothing like him, and it was just a face—nothing more," she replied. "He had been such a doubting Thomas before that happened. Needless to say, he believed the stories a bit more after that incident."

More than one apparition has been seen in the restaurant,

and no one knows exactly who they are. According to one psychic who visited the Grey Moss Inn, the foundation of the building belonged originally to a church. She could see a group of people as they sat in what she described as church pews. She had the distinct impression that Mormons had once wanted to settle in the area. Though the church building was no longer there, was its faithful congregation from the past still coming here to worship?

"Even when I say things are calm and uneventful here in the restaurant, they're not," Nell continued.

"I'll be sitting in the office when I am the only one here," she continued. "And I'll feel this strange need to scoot my chair up closer to the desk. I feel this sense of someone needing to get by me and then think to myself, *wait, there isn't anyone else here*."

Wherever there is a good ghost story, there is a paranormal investigator hot on its trail. Eddie Hill of After Dark Paranormal in San Antonio had come to the Grey Moss Inn with his team to see what activity they could capture with their array of technical tools. During one of their investigations, they set up motion-triggered photography equipment and watched from the porch as several flashes went off inside the restaurant. Confident they had captured something anomalous on film, they reviewed the pictures and found that there was no obvious explanation for the cameras having gone off.

One of the greatest frustrations among investigators is experiencing paranormal phenomena without the ability to record it for everyone else to see. Scientific tools are invaluable, and there are indeed times when we get lucky and catch something with it, but unexplained things can and do happen that science has not yet been able to prove. Does that mean the phenomenon we're experiencing doesn't really exist? No. In my view, it is an indication that science needs to evolve just as our theories and perceptions have evolved since the dawn of human existence.

No one piece of equipment is the say-all-end-all answer. Everything we do in the paranormal field is purely experimental.

Why not begin creating different equations to determine what the final result will be? That is exactly what Eddie and After Dark Paranormal did. Christine Sollers is a psychic sensitive who works with the team, and on her very first visit to the Grey Moss Inn, she indicated that the energetic environment was a bit too much for her and she would not be staying. She did, however, return on other scheduled visits to the restaurant and would eventually relay some interesting impressions about the property to Nell.

As she entered the kitchen, Christine felt as though that space was occupied by a male spirit who was not very pleasant. Oddly enough, the kitchen has always been an area where a lot of freak accidents happen. Glasses sitting securely on their shelves have often flown into the air before smashing into pieces on the floor. A pot of boiling water once spilled onto a cook with no apparent explanation. Christine felt as though the presence in the kitchen was an angry spirit that didn't like others being in his space.

In further discussions with Eddie Hill, he described a bizarre incident that happened as Nell escorted him to the wine cellar.

"The door to the wine cellar was locked," he said, "and as Nell went to open it with her key we heard what sounded like glass hitting the ground. As she opened the door, we saw about five bottles on the floor that had broken. One of them was still intact and was rolling straight toward us."

I imagine it would become rather frustrating for a restaurant owner to have things like this happen, not just because it indicates something paranormal may be happening, but because having to replace glasses and bottles of wine tends to add to the cost of running a business. However, Nell doesn't seem to be fazed by the Grey Moss Inn ghosts. She is content to have them around, and accepts that ghosts are a part of her everyday life.

A portrait of an unknown woman hangs on the wall in the main dining room. It has hung in the restaurant for years, and Nell has always thought that there might have been another portrait of someone underneath that of the woman. It would be impossible to verify without destroying it, though, so she never paid much attention to it.

One evening, a group of women seated in the dining room near the portrait mentioned to Nell that she thought she saw a man faintly standing in the background of it. Luckily, they had brought a digital camera with them and had offered to take a picture. The viewfinder clearly showed the man in the portrait just before a photograph was taken, but once the picture was stored and reviewed in the camera, he was no longer there.

When Eddie Hill and his wife came to the restaurant for dinner a short time later, Nell asked him to take another series of pictures. He snapped six consecutive shots; the first five showed nothing out of the ordinary, but the sixth was a success. The man only a few people had noticed and had been unable to photograph finally appeared in a picture. Who was he, and why was he visible only part of the time? No one has yet been able to offer an explanation.

"My physical self makes space for the spirits here. My higher self is aware of them being around as well, and I just carry on with what I need to do," said Nell.

When in south Texas, visit the Grey Moss Inn for a wonderful dining experience, and remember—it's what's both on and *off* the menu that just might keep you coming back for more.

Spotlight on Ghosts: Ghost Tracks of San Antonio

This is perhaps one of the most well-known ghost legends in the San Antonio area, and while some disagree on what is actually happening at the "ghost tracks," it is difficult to dismiss the story altogether. It all began between the 1930s and 1940s when a school bus full of children approached an intersection of road and railway in a nondescript San Antonio neighborhood. The bus stalled while crossing the tracks and the driver was unable to get the engine up and running again before a train quickly approached.

Realizing the danger he and the children were in, the driver urged them all to exit the bus as quickly as possible to reach safety. Unfortunately, the train collided with the bus before most of the children had the chance to make their getaway, and several of them perished. Over the decades since the incident, many people have visited the tracks in hopes of encountering something paranormal.

While it is never a good idea to park on any railroad track, visitors to the area have put their cars in neutral and sat at this intersection. Some visitors say that their vehicles were inexplicably moved off of the tracks as if being pushed out of harm's way. It became a popular idea to assume that the spirits of the children lost long ago to the bus accident were indeed protecting these individuals by collectively pushing them off the tracks. To test their theories, some people would place baby powder on the bumpers of their cars and discover tiny fingerprints in the dust following the experiment.

It is sad to think that the spirits of the children lost in the accident might still be in the area, constantly reliving the incident in the experiments of others. On the other hand, it can be comforting to believe that, should the same fate befall your vehicle as did the school bus on the ghost tracks of San Antonio, there are several souls keeping watch over you who just might come to your rescue to make sure you arrive safely on the other side.

CHAPTER 29

The Alamo
SAN ANTONIO

**Chapel on
the grounds of
the Alamo
*(Sue Slaughter)***

I COULDN'T VERY WELL WRITE A BOOK about paranormal encounters in Texas without including one of the state's most recognizable symbols—the Alamo. Whether people know the exact history of the Alamo or not, most of us recognize the name. It is a place I deeply respect.

I had never been to the Alamo before moving from Rhode Island to Texas in August 2007, but I had often heard that visiting the shrine was something all Texans had to do at least once in their lifetimes. Friends and family had described it to me as an educational experience, but also a solemn and spiritual one as well.

Allen and I met up with his father and stepmother for a weekend in San Antonio to introduce them to their new grandchildren, my twin daughters Madison and Jordyn. We didn't have a whole lot of time to see everything we wanted to, but as we discussed the schedule, Allen and I believed it would be a good experience to see the Alamo and share a piece of Texas' history with the girls.

Before we left for San Antonio, I did what I always do prior to visiting any new place—I pulled up the history and tried to somehow envision the events that made it so important in the past as well as the role it might play now and in the future. Texas is a state unlike any other, in that I have never before experienced the level of pride I have found in those who call Texas home. There are more state flags flying alongside the American flag than I have seen anywhere else. I have often mentioned to Allen, a native Texan, that this state is really a world all its own. He usually just nods and smiles at me in agreement.

The Alamo is an intrinsic part of Lone Star history. It began as Misión San Antonio de Valero in 1724 and served as a place where Spanish missionaries would educate and convert the Indian people. It was used in that capacity for nearly seventy years. In 1793, the Indians were given the land from the five missions throughout Texas when Spanish officials decided that the missions would no longer be used for religious purposes.

Troops fighting in the Mexican War of Independence took up residence at the mission in the early 1800s and nicknamed it the Alamo, which translates to "cottonwood" in Spanish. Some say that a nearby cluster of cottonwood trees was the inspiration behind the new name, though others believe it is simply because the men wished to name the mission after their hometown, Alamo del Parras, Coahuila.

For ten years during the Mexican struggle for independence, the Spanish, Mexican, and rebel militaries occupied the Alamo. In December 1835, during the Texas Revolution, Texian and Tejano volunteers won out in a five-day battle against Mexican troops led by General Marín Perfecto de Cós. The Mexicans were ultimately forced to surrender and the volunteers defending the site held their position. General Antonio López de Santa Anna advanced on the Alamo with his army on February 23, 1836, and for thirteen days the battle raged. The Texian and Tejano men fought a good fight, but the battle was lost and Santa Anna took control of the Alamo on March 6. While the exact number of casualties from the siege of the Alamo varies, it is estimated that nearly two hundred Texans perished and at least six hundred Mexicans (if not a great deal more) lost their lives.

Today, the old mission chapel and "long barracks" are the only remaining original structures at the site predating the Texas Revolution. The mission itself is gone, but the history is alive and well at the state's most visited historic site.

Paranormal investigations of the property are not allowed, as it is a dedicated shrine to the many who perished there. This is not to say that stories of phenomena have not originated at the site— quite the contrary. The first of many paranormal events occurred after Santa Anna and a majority of his men advanced toward modern-day Houston shortly after the siege of the Alamo. Santa Anna ordered one thousand troops to stay behind in San Antonio to control the rebel forces. In April 1836, Santa Anna was captured by Sam Houston and his men; in an attempt at retaliation, Santa Anna ordered the remainder of his troops in San Antonio to completely destroy the Alamo. As these men approached, six apparitions materialized at the mission doors and commanded that they cause no harm to the mission, frightening the men away.

Assigned with the task of destroying the mission by Santa Anna, Colonel Sanchez was undeterred and sent a group of men to destroy the long barracks. Once again, an apparition appeared to dissuade them. The spirit of a tall man with large balls of fire in each of his two outstretched hands rose from the building and hovered over the men. They quickly retreated, unable and unwilling to complete their assigned task.

When the Alamo was overtaken, the bodies of those who defended it were burned on the property, leading some to believe that their souls had combined into the spiritual forces that continued to defend the site.

Changes and repairs to both the barracks and the chapel began shortly after Texas was annexed into the United States in 1846, and the city of San Antonio began to utilize the complex as their police headquarters and jailing facility. It didn't take long for the prisoners and staff to complain about seeing strange shadows and hearing disembodied moans. San Antonio's politicians eventually moved the facilities off-site as a result.

Today, there are more apparitions reportedly wandering the grounds than can accurately be numbered, but several of them make repeat appearances. The ghost of a small, blonde-haired boy is often seen in the area that now houses the gift shop, though he also walks around the rest of the complex. For one reason or another, his apparition is most often seen on the grounds during the first few weeks of February.

The basement of the mission, which is now mostly used for storage, has also played host to ghostly experiences. Staff members have often felt as though someone were creeping up behind them while working. When they turn to see who might be approaching, the apparition of an Indian man is seen as he quickly steps backward through the wall and disappears. Employees have naturally become reluctant to enter the basement for fear of a repeat encounter with this entity.

Unable to conduct a formal investigation of the property, I decided that it might be helpful to invite a "sensitive" to go along with me and my family on our visit. I contacted a local associate of mine whose abilities have impressed me in the past and asked her if she would be willing to relay her impressions of the grounds. She agreed, but does not wish to be named. We'll simply refer to her as Laura.

With Laura accompanying our family for the visit, we hoped that she would be able to describe for us anything she might sense or feel in regard to paranormal activity. She was fairly quiet as we first began to wander the complex, but as we approached the long barracks she became quite sullen.

"Are you picking up on something?" I asked.

"An overwhelming sense of sadness and defeat," she began. "I see a small group of women crying; a few of them with small children. I don't know for sure who they are, but I get the sense that they are connected to some of the men that lost their lives here."

That thought made me instantly sympathetic, as I looked at my girls and wondered what it must have been like for the families of the men who died at the Alamo. The battles that took place here must have devastated those who were left behind to grieve for the loss of their loved ones.

"Someone wants us to go into the chapel," said Laura.

As we followed her in, we all seemed to feel an automatic reverence. Even my little girls were well-behaved without my having to instruct them to be calm and quiet. There were fewer than a dozen other visitors in the chapel that afternoon. While we were slightly disappointed at not being able to take photographs within the building, we still felt privileged to be allowed in to see it along with the relics still encased inside.

After twenty or so minutes had passed, Laura pulled Allen and me aside and told us that she saw the apparition of a young man, probably in his mid-twenties, sitting on a ledge just below one of the windows near the ceiling.

"He likes watching the people who come in," she said. "He's looked at me and smiled a couple of times in the past minute or so."

"So he actually sees us and knows we are all here?" asked Allen.

"Yes, but I don't get the impression that he ever comes down from that ledge to observe. He may not be there every day, but he's there now and it seems like he truly enjoys people visiting."

"Do you know who he might be?" I asked.

"No, I don't get a name or even if he himself lived or died here," said Laura.

We spent more time walking through the chapel, but Laura did not receive any more impressions and we decided it would be nice to walk the grounds outside for awhile.

The entire complex is beautifully landscaped and maintained, obviously very well-cared for by those assigned with the task. The volunteers who give their time to preserve and educate others about such an important piece of Texas history truly touch my heart.

It is no wonder that a great deal of residual energy still resides at the Alamo; with such a tumultuous past and loss of life, it certainly has reason to be haunted. Other visitors undoubtedly feel the same respect and reverence for this historic site as we did on our visit. Perhaps one day the souls who still roam the grounds and buildings will move on and leave the past behind them. As for now, they remain and continue to touch the lives of all who remember the Alamo.

Spotlight on Ghosts: La Llorona

What could be more hauntingly eerie than the sound of a wailing woman, moving along the banks of rivers and creeks in search of her children? The legend of La Llorona has spread all over the world, and several versions have her haunting the state of Texas.

Hispanic cultures throughout the south have long known, and long feared, the legend of "the weeping woman," the Spanish translation of La Llorona. The legend suggests that her apparition appears to countless individuals in the southwest, dressed in a long white gown and crying uncontrollably. Who is she and why is her restless soul so tormented?

La Llorona is most often described as a young mother, distraught over the loss of her lover and father to her children. In a fit of rage and sadness, she murders her young children and disposes of their bodies in the river before taking her own life. As the evolution of this story has progressed, it is often said that her unfortunate soul was denied entrance into heaven for the gruesome act and her soul is destined to wander the earth forever in search of the souls of those she murdered. While the gender and age of her children differ from version to version, one thing remains the same—La Llorona wanders and cries as she strikes fear in those who believe in her existence.

Shortly after her passing, her apparition repeatedly appeared on the banks of rivers in south Texas and reportedly still does. When night falls, she can be seen floating among the trees and over the water, her long white gown flowing quietly behind her. While she has been said to ruthlessly attack anyone who crosses her path, what is most frightening is her rumored preference for dragging children off in the night to a watery grave. Children are warned not to go out alone in the dark as La Llorona may snatch them up, never to be seen or heard from again.

Other accounts of La Llorona place her on lonely back roads approaching vehicles with an outstretched and withered hand, crying and seemingly in need of help. Drivers have swerved off the road to avoid running her over. Still wearing her long white gown, always weeping, La Llorona is a legend that continues to live on to this day. Perhaps you will see her for yourself on some dark Texas night.

CHAPTER 30

USS *Lexington*
CORPUS CHRISTI

**USS *Lexington*
exterior
(Sue Slaughter)**

IF YOU'VE NEVER BEEN ABOARD an aircraft carrier, you've missed out on a truly awe-inspiring experience. I have always been mystified by how these massive ships stay afloat. I know there is a science to it, but nevertheless, they always impress me each time I have the opportunity to see one.

The USS *Lexington* was built during World War II for the United States Navy as one of twenty-four Essex-class aircraft carriers. Its designated name was to be the USS *Cabot*, but changed to the USS *Lexington* after the ship originally bearing that name was sunk in the Coral Sea. The 910-foot carrier was commissioned in February 1943 and went on to serve the United States longer than any other carrier in our nation's history. The ship was engaged in twenty-one out of twenty-four battles during World War II, and over three hundred of its men were lost in the war.

Unlike its sister ships, the *Lexington* was painted blue, earning it the nickname "the Blue Ghost." The Japanese reported that they had sunk the carrier at least four times, yet it reappeared to engage them in battle once again after every attempt to sink it.

After serving the United States Navy in various capacities, The USS *Lexington* CV-16 was permanently decommissioned on November 8, 1991. The ship was donated to the state of Texas in 1992 and currently operates as the USS Lexington Museum On the Bay. The ship was designated a National Historic Landmark in 2003.

Allen's father and stepmother live in Corpus Christi, so we often have the opportunity of visiting the area. When we mapped out all of the places around town we'd like to see, the USS *Lexington* was at the top of our list. Allen had passed by the ship many times, but he had not yet been able to tour it. Our time schedule was limited, so we knew we had only a matter of hours on the ship before heading to our next destination.

We arrived just as the museum opened at nine o'clock in the morning, and as we drove up the ramp to the parking area adjacent to the ship, Allen reached his hand over to my face and gently pushed my lower jaw upward. I didn't realize that my mouth had been wide open as I sat there in silent awe.

"It's like a skyscraper lying on its side!" I exclaimed.

We parked and stepped out of the car, all staring upward at the massive structure we were about to board. For just a moment, I thought, *Man! I want to join the Navy!* I quickly recovered after remembering how hard military life could be sometimes. Still, if anything would ever have inspired me to join the military, this ship would have been it.

The self-guided tour began as we walked across an aircraft elevator into a hangar bay. Eleven decks and 100,000 square feet of the ship are open to the public to tour. The day I visited,

I happened to be wearing one of my group's t-shirts with The Paranormal Source written across the front of it. We were standing out on the main deck looking at different aircraft when a group of young people noticed my shirt and asked me about it. I told them who we were and what we were about, and they were instantly intrigued.

"Is this ship really haunted?" asked a young man.

"A lot of people believe it is, yes," I answered.

For years, those who have come to tour the USS *Lexington* have reported encounters with an entity in the engine room of the ship referred to simply as "Charlie." He is a polite young man with striking blue eyes, and is always willing to share information on how everything in the engine room operates. His knowledge and demeanor have captivated people so much that they have often spent more time in that one room than anywhere else on the ship. The sailor is described as being dressed in his white uniform and walks with a slight limp in his left leg. Of course, when he is seen it is not immediately apparent that he is a ghost, and visitors are shocked to learn after the tour is over that no volunteer or staff member fitting his description actually mans the engine room.

"I've heard about him before," said one of the young men we'd just met. "They actually have a webcam set up online where you can view a live feed of the engine room. There are several creepy pictures on the Internet of spirits caught on that camera."

I have seen some of those images. One in particular had me staring at it for hours trying to deconstruct it to see if it had been faked. I could find no fault or alteration in the still shot taken from the webcam. It was not the young man in a white uniform as others had reported, but there is most definitely a man in the shot in a WWII uniform. The details are clear in the picture, right down to the buttons on his clothes. I wish I could get my hands on the raw file, just to verify its authenticity. In any case, people from all over the country have relayed stories of encountering a ghost in the engine room.

One of the young women in the group said she thought she was in the middle of a reenactment one day while touring the ship several years back.

"I was walking down one of the narrow hallways toward the front of the ship," she said, "and about five men in uniform ran past me yelling stuff at each other. I just stood there up against the wall and watched them until they were out of sight. None of them even acknowledged that I was there, like they didn't even see me."

"Were they solid? Did any of them brush up against you at all?" I asked.

"They looked solid, but no. None of them touched me at all. They just ran by me and then it was over. They were gone. At first, I thought they were practicing something dramatic for a re-enactment, but it was over so quickly and I didn't see them again so I wasn't sure what happened."

The experience seemed to be more residual than any other type of paranormal phenomenon. It was as if she was seeing a moment in the past play out right in front of her.

Residual activity on the *Lexington* is a common occurrence. The ship's historian, Judith Whipple, has heard several accounts from visitors who have seen apparitions of sailors walking through doorways that are no longer there but that used to lead into other passageways in the past.

Mechanical parts that are no longer operational have been heard as if they were up and running. When volunteers or staff members have gone to inspect the equipment, nothing appears to have changed.

Not every paranormal experience aboard the ship has been residual. Another popular story is that of a painting crew hard at work restoring part of the ship. After having taken a short break, the crew returned to their work area only to find that their job had been completed for them in their absence. People have heard disembodied voices in nearly every section of the ship without seeing anyone around that might be responsible for them.

One of the biggest mysteries to me is the manner in which paranormal specters sometimes appear. Some apparitions seem more fluid and translucent, as if they are floating through the air. Most people believe this is what a ghost would typically look like if they saw one. I know from my own past experience that a ghost can look just as real and solid as you or I, and can even be mistaken for a living, breathing person. Some visitors and staff at the *Lexington* have seen both transparent apparitions and solid ones.

I wonder if it is a matter of choice. In other words, does the spirit of a deceased person decide how he or she will appear to the living? Is it like picking out what outfit to wear, or is it simply a matter of the energy or other resources available to them to manifest? I wonder if we as human beings can even fully perceive them in their entirety to begin with. We have very limited senses, and our physical and biological make up might have a lot to do with how we see and experience the paranormal.

I know that, as investigators, we sometimes become frustrated with the inconsistency and lack of a phenomenon's longevity. I think we have a long way to go before we can even partly understand what is going on around us at any given moment. I have dreams that one day, we'll be able to pick up the phone and call our late relatives as if they had their own direct line, or ask them to come by one afternoon to sit on the couch and talk about how things are in *their* world.

How I would love to walk along the deck of the USS *Lexington* with a sailor who fought in WWII and hear all of his stories of hardship and camaraderie. I'd like to shake his hand and thank him, along with every other military veteran, for their dedication to their country. History would have no holes, and ghosts would not be the feared phantoms in our closets or under our beds. Instead, they could heal our hearts and keep the ones we love accessible to us. I am a dreamer, but it is thoughts like these that keep me searching for answers that have yet to be found, and to turn the "unknown" into the "known."

The USS *Lexington* is one of my favorite places to visit. Whether or not I will ever have the opportunity to experience the phenomena so many others have while aboard, I'll keep on believing that Charlie and the other spirits attached to this amazing piece of U.S. naval history will be there to welcome me upon my return.

Ghosthunting
Travel Guide

Visiting Haunted Sites

North Texas

Amarillo Natatorium/The Nat Bookstore

2705 W. Sixth Avenue
Amarillo, TX 79106
Phone: (806) 220-0251
Website: www.myspace.com/thenatbookstore
Bookstore is open Wed.–Sat. noon to 7 P.M.
For a visit to the ballroom, ask to speak with Branden.

Motley County Jail

709 Main Street
Matador, TX 79244
Phone: (806) 347-2234 (County Courthouse)
Please contact the county courthouse to schedule a visitation time.

Fort Phantom Hill

Located on the east side of FM 600, in Jones County.
Follow FM Road 600 and exit I-20. Go 11 miles north.
Phone: (325) 677-1309
Website: www.fortphantom.org/fort/ftphantm.nsf/home?openpage
Open daily to the public from dawn until dusk.

Lonesome Dove Inn

225 West Main Street
Archer City, TX 76351
Phone: (940) 574-2700
Website: www.lonesomedoveinn.com/index.html
Please call for nightly rates and availability.

Hill House Manor

Located on N. Denton Street
Gainesville, TX 76240
Website: www.hillhousemanor.com

Please e-mail linda@pdslab.com for reservation times and rates.
Exact address is given when a reservation is conflrmed.

Old Alton Bridge

No exact address listed.
Located over Hickory Creek on Copper Canyon Road in Denton
GPS Coordinates: 33°07'46" N, 97°06'15" W
Common area / Open to the public

Bull Ring

112 E. Exchange Avenue
Fort Worth, TX 76164
Phone: (817) 624-2222
Website: www.fortworthstockyards.org/business_page.aspx?fwsy_
id=5&sort=59
Open Wed.–Fri. 8:30 A.M. to 5:00 P.M.
Sat. and Sun. 8:30 A.M. to varying closing time
Closed Mon. and Tues.

Majestic Theatre

1925 Elm Street
Dallas, TX 75201
Phone: (214) 880-0137
Website: www.liveatthemajestic.com
Please contact box offlce for performance dates and times.

Millermore at Dallas Heritage Village

1515 S. Harwood Street
Dallas, TX 75215-1273
Phone: (214) 428-5448
Website: www.dallasheritagevillage.org/VisitorInformation.aspx
Open daily at 1:30 P.M. for public tours.
Admission prices to the park vary by season.

The Iris Theatre/Books & Crannies

209 W. Moore Avenue
Terrell, TX 75160
Phone: (972) 563-5481

Website: www.bookscrannies.com
Open Mon.–Thurs. 10:00 A.M. to 6:00 P.M.
Sat. 10:00 A.M. to 5:00 P.M. Closed Sun.

Catfish Plantation

814 Water Street
Waxahachie, TX 75165
Phone: (972) 937-9468
Website: www.catflshplantation.com
Open Wed.–Sat 11 A.M. to 9 P.M.
Sun. 11 A.M. to 8 P.M.

West Texas

Plaza Theatre

125 Pioneer Plaza
El Paso, TX 79901
Phone: (915) 534-0600
Website:www.theplazatheater.org
Please visit the online calendar for schedule of events.

Gage Hotel

101 Highway 90 West
Marathon, TX 79842
Phone: (432) 386-4205
Website: www.gagehotel.com
Please call for nightly rates and availability.

Cental Texas

Old Fort Concho

630 S. Oakes Street
San Angelo, TX 76903
Phone: (325) 481-2646
Website: www.fortconcho.com
Museum open Mon.–Sat. 9 A.M. to 5 P.M.
Sun. 1 P.M. to 5 P.M.

Admission for adults is $3.00; seniors and military $2.00; students $1.50, children under 6 are free.

Oakwood Cemetery

2124 S. Fifth Street
Waco, TX 76706
Phone: (254) 754-1631
Grounds are open daily to the public from dawn until dusk.

Dead Man's Hole

No exact address listed.
Located 2 miles south of Marble Falls on US 281.
Travel a half mile east on RM 2147 and another half mile south on CR 401.
Common area / Open to the public

Driskill Hotel

604 Brazos Street
Austin, TX 78701
Phone: (512) 474-5911
Website: www.driskillhotel.com
Please call for nightly rates and availability.

Caldwell County Jail Museum

315 E. Market Street
Lockhart, TX 78644-2750
Website: www.lockhart-tx.org/web98/history/caldwellcountymuseum.asp
Open to the public for tours Sat. and Sun. from 1 P.M. to 5 P.M.

Von Minden Hotel

607 Lyons Avenue
Schulenburg, TX 78956
Phone: (979) 743-3716
Website: www.myspace.com/vonmindenhotel
Please call for nightly rates and availability.

East Texas

Oaklea Mansion Bed & Breakfast

407 S. Main Street
Winnsboro, TX 75494
Phone: (903) 342-6051
Website: www.oakleamansion.com
Please call for nightly rates and availability.

Crystals Rock Shop

2136 Roy Road
Tyler, TX 75707
Phone: (903)581-7750
Website: www.freebirdjewelry.net
Open for business Fri. and Sat. from 10 A.M. to 6 P.M.

Dabbs Cemetery

Located in Frankston, TX 75763
Directions: In Frankston, turn on TX 19 and travel southeast toward Neches.
Travel 3 miles and turn right at the green Dabbs Cemetery sign. Continue 2.2
miles to a "Y" in the road. Take the left road and travel 0.8 miles to another
"Y." Take the right road and continue for 0.9 miles. This road will change from
blacktop to dirt. Turn right and after 0.3 miles you will see the cemetery on the
right.
(Directions courtesy of Monetta Alexander Lockey.)
Grounds are open daily to the public from dawn until dusk.

The Grove

405 Moseley Street
Jefferson, TX 75657
Phone: (903) 665-8018
Website: www.thegrove-jefferson.com
Please call for tour times and information.
Admission is $6.00.
Children under the age of 8 are not permitted.

Ghost Train of Jefferson

400 E. Austin Street
Jefferson, TX 75657
Phone: (866) 398-2038
Website: www.jeffersonrailway.com/store/index.php?main_
page=page&id=3&chapter=1
Tickets are $10.00 for adults; $8.00 for seniors (62+); $8.00 for children (3 to
12); children under 3 ride free.

Scottsville Cemetery

Located on the north side of FM 1998
Scottsville, TX 75688
Grounds are open daily to the public from dawn until dusk.

Spaghetti Warehouse

901 Commerce Street
Houston, TX 77002
Phone: (713) 229-9715
Open Sun.–Thurs. 11 A.M. to 10 P.M.
Fri. and Sat. 11 A.M. to 11 P.M.

USS *Texas*

3527 Battleground Road
La Porte, TX 77571
Phone: (281) 479-2431
Website: www.tpwd.state.tx.us/spdest/flndadest/parks/battleship_texas
*Texas Park Wildlife Department employees are instructed not to discuss
paranormal activity aboard the ship.

South Texas

Grey Moss Inn

19010 Scenic Loop Road
Helotes, TX 78023-9209
Phone: (210) 695-8301
Website: www.grey-moss-inn.com/index.html
Open 5 P.M. to 10 P.M. daily, closed on major holidays.

The Alamo

300 Alamo Plaza
San Antonio, TX 78299
Phone: (210) 225-1391
Website: www.theaalamo.org
Open Mon.–Sat. 9:00 A.M. to 5:30 P.M.
Sun. 10:00 A.M. to 5:30 P.M.
Closed Christmas Eve and Christmas Day.
Admission is free.

USS *Lexington*

2914 North Shoreline
Corpus Christi, TX 78402-1116
Phone: (361) 888-4873
Website: www.usslexington.com
Open 7 days a week from 9 A.M. to 6 P.M., Memorial Day through Labor Day
Open 9 A.M. to 5 P.M., Labor Day through Memorial Day
Admission for adults is $12.95; seniors (60+) and active or retired military are
$10.95; children 4 to 12 are $7.95; children under 4 are free.

Additional Haunted Sites

Admiral Nimitz State Historic Site

340 E. Main Street
Fredericksburg, TX 78624

Shadows have been seen walking around the site. Lights go on and off on their own and footsteps are heard when no one is around.

Airy Mount Bed & Breakfast

1819 Polk Street
Burnet, TX 78611

Ghostly sounds of children playing on the property are often reported. Guests have also witnessed shadowy apparitions moving around their rooms.

Ashton Villa House Museum

2328 Broadway Street
Galveston, TX 77550-4642

Former resident Bettie Brown is said to haunt the home. Witnesses report seeing her apparition and hearing her play the piano. She is most often seen standing at the top of the home's staircase.

Austin Pizza Garden

6266 W. Highway 290
Austin, TX 78799

Apparitions have been seen in the restaurant along with silverware inexplicably moving on its own. Strange drops in temperature and the sound of footsteps have also been reported.

Concordia Cemetery

3700 E. Yandell Drive
El Paso, TX 79903

After one hundred and fifty years and sixty thousand burials, this cemetery is rumored to be extremely haunted. The sounds of children playing, muf ed conversations, and hoof beats are often heard.

Emily Morgan Hotel

705 E. Houston Street
San Antonio, TX 78205

The seventh and twelfth oors of the hotel are home to several apparitions, as is the basement. Electrical equipment often malfunctions with no apparent cause.

The Excelsior House

211 W. Austin
Jefferson, TX 75657

The ghost of Diamond Bessie is often seen, as well as headless apparitions and that of a woman holding a baby. Rocking chairs will also rock on their own.

Fort Worth Zoo

1989 Colonial Parkway
Fort Worth, TX 76110

The apparition of an unknown woman is seen walking near the café. A man killed by one of the zoo's elephants is said to haunt the elephant and zebra exhibit areas.

Heritage Park

1581 Chaparral Street
Corpus Christi, TX 78401

Four homes located in the park have activity ranging from touching, noises, slamming of doors, and the sightings of apparitions.

Hotel Faust

240 S. Seguin Avenue
New Braunfels, TX 75130

Common occurrences include water and lights turning on and off on their own, and doors opening and closing on their own.

Houston Public Library

500 McKinney Street
Houston, TX 77002

People have heard a violin playing in the rotunda and in the "Texas" room. It is believed to be haunted by the ghost of a janitor who died in the 1930s.

Imaginarium of South Texas

5300 San Dario, Suite 505
Laredo, TX 78041

The building is located on a site that was once reportedly a morgue. Shadows can be seen, disembodied voices are heard, and inexplicable cold spots are felt.

Killough Monument

FM 3411
Near Jacksonville, TX

Several families were reportedly killed by Caddo Indians in the 1830s. Visitors have often seen an Indian chief and his horse here, accompanied with an overwhelming onset of fear.

La Lomita Mission

107 FM 1016
Mission, TX 78572

Activity seen at the mission includes the sighting of several apparitions in robes and disembodied voices seemingly engaged in prayer.

The Lizard Lounge

2424 Swiss Avenue
Dallas, TX 75204

Formerly known as the Grand Crystal Palace Theatre, this building is now haunted by a mysterious "man in black" who is seen in the old seating area.

Menger Hotel

204 Alamo Plaza
San Antonio, TX 78205

According to the hotel's director of public relations, there are at least thirty-two different apparitions roaming the hotel. They roam the lobby, halls, and inside the guest rooms.

Miss Molly's Bed & Breakfast

109 W. Exchange Avenue, Suite 200
Fort Worth, TX 76106

Poltergeist activity has been reported along with the sightings of several apparitions in every room of the B&B.

Panhandle-Plains Historical Museum

2503 Fourth Avenue
Canyon, TX 79015

Full-body apparitions are commonly seen, and visitors have often complained of sudden severe headaches and the onset of inexplicable panic.

Permian Playhouse

310 W. 42nd Street
Odessa, TX 79764

Moving cold spots and the feeling of being touched is common here. Disembodied voices are also heard.

Spring Creek Park

15012 Brown Road
Tomball, TX 77375

Modern reports include seeing Civil War–era soldiers, muf ed sounds of explosions, and hot and cold spots that defy explanation.

Thistle Hill House Museum

1509 Pennsylvania Avenue
Fort Worth, TX 76104-2028

Apparitions of a man and a woman have both been seen walking the grand staircase of the house. Disembodied voices and music are also heard coming from the ballroom.

Wunsche Bros. Café & Saloon

103 Midway
Spring, TX 77373

Reportedly haunted by "Uncle Charlie," a bitter old man who lived on the upper oor of the building before his death in the 1930s.

ACKNOWLEDGMENTS

I have to begin with thanking my mother and father, for indulging my stories about the "people in the basement." I'm glad they are still there to keep watch over you in my absence. I will forever be indebted to Chris and Nancy Peterson, whose knowledge and patience molded me in my paranormal infancy. Thank you, Rosemary Ellen Guiley, for your constant support and unwavering belief in me. You are everything I aspire to be as a writer. I appreciate my editor John Kachuba and those at Clerisy Press for answering my never-ending list of questions. To everyone who contributed photographs and information for this book, you have my sincerest thanks. Thanks to RED, whose music kept me motivated and inspired. Last but not least, my deepest gratitude goes to my wonderful team of investigators with The Paranormal Source, Inc.—Jerry Bowers, "They See Me" John Melchior, Buffy Clary, Victoria Dupree, James and Mary Hampton, Adam Norton and Gabriela Kelley-Norton, and Sheri Smith. You are all what makes working in this field an amazing adventure.

About the Author

APRIL SLAUGHTER and her husband Allen are the founders and Executive Directors of The Paranormal Source, Inc. (www.paranormalsource.com)—a nonprofit research and education corporation based in Dallas, Texas. April spent three years as a staff journalist for *TAPS Paramagazine*, published by TAPS Parapublications, LLC, and contributed several feature articles on various paranormal phenomena, as well as her recurring column entitled *Ghost Hunting State-by-State*. April is an avid paranormal researcher and investigator currently working on projects involving Electronic Voice Phenomena & Instrumental Transcommunication (EVP-ITC) along with several upcoming publishing projects.

April Slaughter, Author
(© Kade Steel Photography)